Fans.

Friends.

Music.

Band.
Fans.
Friends.
Music.

Memoirs of a post-punk fan

Inge van Sombrië

ASPEKT

Author's note:
The band photographs in this book were taken by me or my friends,
unless clearly stated otherwise.

Original title: Band. Fans. Vrienden. Muziek.
Translated from Dutch into English by Inge van Sombrië.

Band. Fans. Friends. Music.

© Inge van Sombrië
© 2023 Aspekt Publishers | Amersfoortsestraat 27, 3769 AD Soesterberg
info@uitgeverijaspekt.nl | www.uitgeverijaspekt.nl

Cover: Lisa Dijkhuizen
Interlining: BeCo DTP-Productions, Epe

ISBN: 9789464870497
NUR: 660

For my lovely friend Rolf, who passed away far too young.
He was a great Comsat fan.

And of course for Mik, Steve, Andy, Kevin, Terry and Simon.

With thanks to (in alphabetical order):

The Armoury Show, The Associates, Bauhaus, The Birthday Party, The Blow Monkeys, The Chameleons, The Church, The Comsat Angels, The (Death) Cult, DAF, The Danse Society, Department-S, Echo and the Bunnymen, Europeans, Fad Gadget, Fehlfarben, Gang of Four, Modern English, Modern Eon, OMD, The Opposition, Palais Schaumburg, Sad Lovers and Giants, Shriekback, Simple Minds, Siouxsie and the Banshees, The Sisters of Mercy, The Sound, Spear of Destiny, Talk Talk, TC Matic, The Teardrop Explodes and The Virgin Prunes,

but also Aztec Camera, Big Country, Blancmange, Depeche Mode, Duran Duran, Fischer-Z, The Fixx, Icehouse, Japan, Orange Juice, Tears for Fears, The The, U2 and Ultravox,

and then all the bands that I forget to put on this list due to my almost-turning-60 forgetfulness,

You made my eighties one big party.

I bought your records, saw your concerts, sat at almost every afternoon sound check, joined you backstage for a drink and a chat, and loved you more than anything.

You were GREAT.

This book is mainly about the band The Comsat Angels, but also a bit about all of them.

It began like this.

I know a Chinese who suffered from haemorrhoids,
It was a torture, goin to the loo
'Till one day he bought a videodeck,
Now he shits for hours
watching technicoloured kungfu

On a wall in the dressing room there was a strange little poem. The place looked worn-out, but that really applied to every dressing room in every 'music temple' in the Netherlands. Here and there words had been scratched out or corrected. Every band had to make their mark, let people know that they played here. I don't know who came up with this rhyme; many musicians had already been in this room, before and after their performance.

The Trojan Horse in The Hague was the setting for my first time backstage with The Comsat Angels. I never could have imagined it at the time, but this evening would lead to a passion and a friendship that still lasts. Over forty years later.

The Comsat Angels (generally shortened to 'Comsats') was an English band that was part of the crop of 'new wave' bands of the late seventies, early eighties. *New wave* (nowadays usually called *post-punk*) was a logical follow-up of the punk that came before it, in the second half of the seventies. Punk was mostly a lot of anger, raging and screaming, and *new wave* was again about music, about more than three chords, and was atmospheric and dark, so you could distinguish yourself from the 'normal' teenager and twenty-something who listened to the charts. It felt exclusive to belong.

When people refer to the eighties and mention pink leg warmers, I always tend to raise my eyebrows. No, absolutely no pink leg warmers, definitely not. Black, heavy and gloomy was the thing in 'my scene'. If you opened a wardrobe, everything was black. We were elitist and a bit arrogant and we felt slightly elevated above the common rabble. We drank 'berries' (berry jenever), dyed our hair black and backcombed it in all directions. But mainly up. We joked that the hole in the ozone layer was caused for the larger part by the can of hair spray we used up every week. Later on, big hair became commonplace in the pink leg warmers brigade, so we called it quits. But let me start at the beginning.

My gig-going life had just begun, earlier that year. I hadn't seen that many concerts yet, but I chose them carefully. Mainly British *new-wave* bands, that was the loot so far.

I was a well-raised, well-behaved schoolgirl, I had never played truant (yes, really), I always did my homework without my mother nagging me, I wore jeans, rode horses, and loved Al Stewart, 10cc and The Babys. And sometimes Neil Diamond.

And then my new life began.

I had already seen the Comsats from afar during the summer, at a festival where I actually went to see something else, and therefore had not paid much attention when they played. But I knew the name. A new friend of mine, whom I had met just two months earlier at the Paradiso, had already been to many more gigs than I had. Because of her wider meet-the-band experience, she acted a bit like a role model for me, and when she said 'nice music, nice guys, they're playing in The Hague next week, come along', I went. It was that simple. And so I ended up at the Horse, stood as always in the front row with my new gig friends and was impressed. And then spoke to the band.

Now that was something. Gee, what an experience. I filled up my diary that same night. It led to gig after gig, year after year, tour after tour. It led to letter after letter, to trips to England outside of gigs, and to staying at the band members' homes. Up to the present day.

But fortunately I have no idea about that at the beginning.

It began like this.

Backstage with The Comsat Angels

(November 1981, from my teenage diary, very detailed)
Tonight I had my first real dressing room conversation, as I had always imagined it. With Mik Glaisher, the drummer of The Comsat Angels.

Dad took me in his car to the Trojan Horse at half past ten, as the band started at eleven. I soon found Claire and the others, in the front row of course. The Comsats played approximately 70 minutes, with two breaks. I don't have any of their records and so I didn't recognise anything during the gig, but I liked it anyway.

I had already seen in the Horse magazine that Steve Fellows, the singer, looks a bit like my old hero John. That resemblance, however, is becoming vague. Steve is also nicer to look at. Then there's Andy Peake, the keyboard player, who everyone fancies, but I don't. Finally, the bass player, Kevin Bacon. Obviously a dull person with a very whimpy appearance. I won't waste many words on the three of them. Except that Steve wore horrible sandals, and said between songs during the gig that most people would be embarrassed to wear them, but they were a gift from his father.

Afterwards we went to the dressing room. Just like at the Paradiso earlier this year, this was simply a case of going in, because nobody besides us was interested. And no one from the Horse tried to stop us. I started by asking autographs, first Andy, because he was closest. I had only brought a white inner sleeve with which I hoped to deceive them. I pretended this was the inner sleeve of their first album, *Waiting for a Miracle*, which I don't have (yet). Andy didn't fall for it and immediately asked where the rest of the record was. When it turned out that I didn't have an outer sleeve, let alone an LP, he acted a bit indignant. I said that I was really going to buy the album soon and his face said 'you'd better' and he thought I should do it tomorrow.

Well, then I walked over to Kevin, who wrote his name on the inner sleeve with a little cross underneath as a 'personal touch', he said. Then to Steve. He's really nice to look at and nice to talk to. According to Claire, he is very shy and private, but I didn't really notice that. I liked him. When I asked him to write more than just his autograph, he drew a house with eyes under his name and the words 'Do the empty house'. I don't know what that nonsense means, but oh well. And then it happened.

Drummer Mik Glaisher

Claire, Ronald and Nahna were already busy talking to keyboard player Andy, so Annemarie and I headed for drummer Mik, although then we still thought his name was Mick. After he wrote on the sleeve 'I think Inge is a real deadringer' (what does that word mean?), a wonderful conversation started between the three of us, just great. It began with him noticing my Modern Eon badge and asking if I liked that band. Well, you can say that again, I absolutely love them. It turned out that he had actually just met Danny from Modern Eon, who had come to see a Comsat performance. Danny had told him that their band's drummer had left them because he broke his wrists, and that they now had a new drummer. Mik had never seen them play, but knew their album and thought it was a bit disappointing. That is, he liked the songs themselves, but he didn't agree with the production. Well, I don't understand things like that. He had also not been able to see them at Rotterdam Newpop, the festival this summer, because then they both played on different stages.

I saw my chance and asked if he knew Fischer-Z, after which he pulled a face. Well, Annemarie and I, being great fans, immediately took action and gave him hell, so to speak. We explained that with English people his reaction is quite common. That Fischer-Z is very popular in the Netherlands, but not in England. He thought that they brought nothing new, that they were rather ordinary. But he had never seen them live and knew no songs at all. In the end he promised that when he got home he would borrow one of their LPs to listen to, because maybe he had overlooked things.

While we were chatting away like this, Steve half listened in. Suddenly he also opened his mouth and asked who we were talking about. I said 'Fischer-Z' and he immediately went 'oh, yuck'. So I blurted out 'I hate you', and he pretended to flinch with his hands in front of his face and said 'sorry', the joker. Mik told Steve that he was so 'impressed by their enthusiasm' that he had decided to listen to this band again.

Mik then asked how long I've been speaking English because I do it so well, he said. Since about the age of 12, I think. He'd noticed that everyone here speaks English so well, or at least knows some English. We have to, I said, because no one else in the world speaks Dutch. He said most people think that the English are lazy, but they are not encouraged at school at all. They only receive lessons in foreign languages for half an hour twice a week. We here in the Netherlands, I said, learn French, German and English and in some schools even Spanish. He thought that was great and he said that the command of English in Germany is already a lot less than here, and in France they can do it, but they refuse to. If you ask the French something, they will answer in French, Mik said.

So I suggested that he should learn Dutch. Oh, but I've already started, he said with a straight face. He went into a shop to buy matches, but he had heard how to say that in Dutch, namely that you want a 'vuurtje' (literally: a small fire). So he had asked: 'Can I have a future?' Ha ha, yes, the words do sound almost identical. The right Dutch word is 'lucifers', Mik. He tried his best to pronounce it correctly, but he couldn't. So I took the back of (how coincidental) a matchbook that was lying around and wrote it down, and he tried to say it again. It was more or less OK. He remarked intelligently that 'lucifers' also means devils and then put the piece of paper in his breast pocket for safe keeping.

Then I saw some rhyme written on a wall, which read: 'Once upon a time there was a Chinese man who suffered from... (difficult word, I forget) and it hurt so much,' etc. I didn't know what the word meant, so I asked Mik about it. He was a bit shy at first and said it was very embarrassing and very hard to explain, but when I insisted, he mumbled something like 'rectum'. So I said, 'I see,' and he took courage and said something about veins swelling up and hurting when you sit on them. Haemorrhoids then. Annemarie and I said the Dutch word 'aambeien' in unison, and I fished the piece of cardboard out of his breast pocket again and wrote the word under 'lucifers'. I remarked that it was a bit strange that out of all available Dutch words he learned precisely these two, but well, it happened that way.

By now it was 5 to 1, and Dad was supposed to pick me up at 1 o'clock. There was no way I could keep him waiting in the car, so I was getting ready to leave when Annemarie asked for an address. Mik actually responded with 'mine or the management's?', so that became both. I asked when they thought to return to Holland, because then I can ask him about his experiences with Fischer-Z. Claire, standing nearby, suddenly thought I could write to him with advice on Fischer-Z. Mik promised to do his homework and let me quiz him next time. OK, Mik!

Oh dear, it's almost 3.30 am now and I have to get up at 9.30 am, because I'm going to Amsterdam. Bye.

(Two days later)
There was a review in the paper yesterday. I think it's more or less correct. I am a bit surprised at the formal language though.

'The quartet from Sheffield has already performed several times in our country this year, but is still definitely worth paying attention to. In fact, it is a group that cannot be heard often enough. A group that is in a strong upward movement and therefore needs to be closely monitored. The Comsat Angels do not indulge in such frills as outward appearance, poses and the like, but say it with music, or rather, with sound. They have mastered the art of omission down to the last detail. That's why the instrumentation – the accents, the tempo changes, the melodic twists – in all its refined simplicity is so enormously effective. Rhythmically dynamic, somewhat stately atmospheric music with a constant sense of threat, which is filled in with spatial insight by the guitarist and the keyboard player.

The Comsat Angels always had some difficulty conveying their emotional drive during concerts. Yesterday it was therefore mainly about getting those suspected live qualities confirmed. The group succeeded with flying colours. The Comsat Angels were already a band well worth seeing. Last night they were too focused to cause boredom even for a moment.'

(A week later)
I have written an unimaginable number of letters in the past few days. To Nahna and Claire, and to Mik. I am a little nervous about the latter, and also very curious about the result of that letter. I'm a little worried that I'm imposing, that I'm writing too soon, that he won't even have time to catch his breath and possibly listen to the LP. But I comfort myself with the thought that it may take two weeks for the letter to reach him.

Singer Steve, drummer Mik, keyboard player Andy, bass player Kevin

Today Mum said something I have been thinking about too, although we clearly have very different opinions on the subject. I had told her that I want to go on tour with Modern Eon when they come to the Netherlands again. At first she didn't believe me, thought it was a whim, but in recent days I think she's starting to realise that it's more than just a fantasy. Although I'm not sure if I'd really dare to go, but we'll see when the time comes.

Anyway, today I said something about it again and mum said: 'When you say that I always have the feeling that you should go on the pill'. That in itself makes no sense, it's not as if you are automatically required to act like a groupie when you go on tour with a band. 'Pop stars' (as mum always puts it) may have that image of 'taking back a girl after every gig', but I've already clearly noticed that that's not always the case. Well, Duran maybe, I can see them do it, but not immediately the Comsats, for example. Although you could be wrong about that: according to Claire, Jacqueline (an ex-friend of hers and a very experienced groupie) went with someone from Modern Eon after the Paradiso gig.

But to get back to me: basically I can't see anything happening, but if Alix from Modern Eon is as cute in real life as when I dream about him (probably not, but I assume he will always be nice, like he was in August), well, you never know. But that would have nothing to do with being an artist. I just like Alix as a person, and I was also rather charmed by Mik last Friday, and also found Steve quite attractive.

Well, I'm now thinking all sorts of strange things, so I don't know, but going on the pill, oh well, why not, it can't hurt. I just don't think I need it for after gigs. Why would I suddenly jump into bed with all these musicians? They're just ordinary people, I'm convinced of that by now.

(A week later)
Last Saturday I went to Amsterdam with Claire and we had a lot of fun, despite the fact that it kept raining. I actually went there in search of Comsat singles. I have already found three singles in a record shop at home. Ridiculous, we went to three or four shops, but no Comsat records. One can buy their stuff in the sticks, but not in Amsterdam!

By the way, that 'Do the empty house' Steve wrote on my inner sleeve wasn't just a spontaneous thought, it's the title of a single. So I have learned.

I told Claire everything I wrote to Mik. She said she might see Mik at the U2 concert in London, because several Comsats are going there (she remained in the dressing room last week after I had to leave, and they had talked to her about this gig) and then she would say hello to him for me. She would probably also write to him and tell him how much I liked him. She thinks he will probably write back, because he is the type, and I rather think so, too. But she said that the Comsats had continued their tour into Germany after the Netherlands, so no idea when he comes home.

I asked her what she thought of that following a tour business and she said: 'Go on the pill. If your mother offers, always take it, but it is absolutely not necessary. After all, they have groupies for that and moreover, bands are usually completely exhausted after a gig anyway'.

The inner sleeve with autographs, now with LP

On groupies

Babylonian confusion

Let me start with a language issue. I have often felt terribly offended when someone said to me, 'Oh, you're a groupie!' 'No!' I would exclaim angrily, 'not at all. I'm just a really big fan who follows the band.'

It took me a few years to understand that we are not dealing here with short-sighted people who like to offend other people, but with a persistent misunderstanding of language.

The Dutch language has for decades been adopting English words with great enthusiasm and slowly changing them into Dutch words. That in itself is not a problem, as long as you keep in mind that the meaning of such a word often changes with it. That's what happened here, too. The word 'groupie', spoken by a Brit, still makes me defensive, but when a Dutch person asks me if I'm a groupie, I cheerfully say: 'I most certainly am'.

English

What is the difference? In English, groupies are girls who always hang around at sound checks, in dressing rooms and in hotels, hoping a band member will take them back to his room for a one-night stand. They target (hopefully soon to be) famous musicians. The more bands they've been with, the more famous these bands are, the more important the groupies are, the better their self-esteem, and the prouder they are of their track record.

They are present in all places where there is a chance to encounter the band, they wear quite provocative clothing (short skirts, fishnet tights, transparent tops) and are covered in piles of make-up. Groupies usually work solo, although duos also exist. More fun, right? And then they are not necessarily competing with each other, because each band has at least three members, so there is plenty of choice.

'If you get the drummer, you're having a bad night'
Groupies use a ranking system. It's best to score the singer. If you've spent the night in the bed of a singer who's going to make it big in the foreseeable future, that's definitely something to brag about. Second option, less ideal, but still acceptable, is the guitarist. Keyboard player or bass player is also OK'ish, but the drummer? You'd better not even confess to that, because you might get a pitying look from a fellow groupie.

Dressed in a belt
At the Paradiso there is an in-house groupie, who is always everywhere we hang out, too. Her name is Jacqueline, but to make things easier for English bands, she calls herself Jackie. Jackie is a given, Paradiso's resident groupie. She is quite pretty, has a nice figure and is always present. I don't think she's very picky, but she is definitely very experienced. After a few visits to the dressing room I begin to recognise who she is targeting tonight. And most of the time things go exactly as she planned. Men don't make a fuss when a beautiful girl offers herself after all.

Her outfits are completely in the style of the moment, all black, super short skirts, fishnet tights, leather boots with high heels, and lots of belts. And she has professionally backcombed, long, very blond hair. On one occasion her skirt is so short and her belt so wide that someone from the band who is in the dressing room at that moment remarks: 'Jackie is dressed in a belt today'.

Acquaintances
In addition to Jackie, there are two other groupies that we regularly bump into. Well, groupies… Esther and Linda are trying very hard, but they have some start-up problems. Jackie dismissively says that they are not 'professional' enough to call themselves groupies.

When we first encounter them at a Comsat gig, we've seen them in a dressing room twice before. In both cases they went home unsuccessfully. Apparently, picking up a band member is harder than you might think. So, we know each other by sight, but now they discover that we have known the Comsats for quite some time. They more or less assume that we have already divided the gentlemen amongst ourselves. Checking just to be sure:

    Esther/Linda: Are you going to the dressing room after the gig?
    We: Yes.
    E/L: Do you know them well?
    We: Yes, for over two years now, and we've seen them about 15 times.
    E/L: And do you sleep with them?
    We: No.
    E/L: Great, then we will!

We wish the ladies the best of luck. After the concert they hurry up the stairs to the dressing room. But why the band are so friendly to us, while we don't do anything to earn it, is incomprehensible.

Dutch

In Dutch, the word groupie means little more than: super fan, buys all the records, goes to as many gigs as possible, thinks about the band all the time and probably has posters on her bedroom wall. If that is the definition, then I wholeheartedly plead 'guilty'.

The confusing thing is that we are always exactly where the groupies, in the English sense, are too. We are also at every sound check of every band, because our motto is: 'Is it a new-wave band from the UK? Then we're going.'

We also try to go to the dressing room after every single gig, which usually goes well, and sometimes we go out with the band afterwards. So we know the groupies, and the groupies know us. But we are not in competition with them. We want a nice chat, a drink, maybe a drag of a passing joint, but that's about it. We are just curious about 'the people behind the music'.

Oh yes, and can we maybe get a management address so we can send letters and cards to the band, and look up their manager with burning questions next time we're in London? Which is often.

As a rule, the bands sense flawlessly which girls are groupies and which are not. We are rarely if ever 'harassed' in a dressing room. Occasionally a bit of a shame.

Under an umbrella

One day four of us are waiting outside a hall under two umbrellas. An indoor festival is held in the hall and the Comsats are one of the main attractions. It's raining, it's pouring, and we do have a little money, but we'd prefer to be on the guest list instead of buying a ticket. So we are waiting for the well-known band van to arrive. We are waiting under those umbrellas for seven (yes, you read that right, seven) hours. Every now and then we go to a café, in pairs, to warm up and drink hot tea, and then we stand guard again.

People who pass us for the fourth time begin to whisper and giggle, and say just too loudly: 'See them over there? Tsss, groupies'.

'No!!', I thought at the time. Later I understood the problem. Oh well, what do common Dutch people know about the music scene? Yeah, it's fine, we're groupies. But especially of the Comsats.

To be clear, when in this book I use the word groupie, it is always in the English sense.

The second year, make or break

The year following our first meeting is decisive. Are the Comsat Angels a keeper, will it be a band to see once in a while, or is there more to it? It can still go either way. There are so many great new bands that come to play here. I never heard back from Mik, by the way.

In the summer of 1982 the Comsats play at Parkpop, a new festival in The Hague, a free event too, so I round up the troops and the four of us go.

I enjoy the performance, which is really, really good. And this time I can say this wholeheartedly, because I now have two LPs at home, which I play often. It took some getting used to, especially the second album, *Sleep No More*. That music is melancholy, gloomy and somewhat depressing, quite different from the rest of my modest record collection, but as a teenager you're flexible and you try everything, so I persevered and now know all the music well. The beautiful memory of my adventure at the Trojan Horse is of course also firmly set in my memory.

After the Comsat performance, we sneak through the bushes on the festival site and immediately find ourselves backstage. In the early eighties, there is hardly anything that can pass for security. The world is considerably safer and more innocent than it is today, and the idea of strict security at gigs has yet to be invented. Crazy things haven't happened yet.

My diary says that 'Claire has already been smuggled in by a roadie and is just walking back to the field together with Mik, intending to pick up Nahna, Ronald and me, when we've just managed to get there ourselves. Mik immediately hugs Nahna and me. Second miracle: the first thing he says is that he has actually listened to Fischer-Z.

Singer-guitarist Steve Fellows at Parkpop 1982

He doesn't like it, but that doesn't matter, he has remembered and listened to it.'

All bands have their own trailer backstage, which serves as a dressing room, and we go in with Mik and stay there for a long time. Nahna gets into conversation with Andy, while Ronald and I have a great time with Mik. I promise Mik I will write him a second letter and he promises to write back.

A few days after Parkpop the band are off to Hilversum to record some songs for *Götterdämmerung 2000*, a new tv programme about new-wave music. The Comsats on Dutch television for the first time! We are vicariously proud of that. And they were also on the cover of OOR music magazine this year, so it would seem that their career is going in the right direction.

Other big news this year is that we're finally getting cable tv. From one day to the next we go from two channels to no less than fourteen. In addition to the familiar Netherlands 1 and 2, we suddenly have access to twelve foreign channels. Two Flemish-Belgian, two French-Belgian, three German, BBB1 and BBC2, and ITV. And, very essential, Music Box and SKY Channel, which show lots of music videos. Yes! Finally I can watch 'Top of the Pops' myself and many other well-known English music programmes. But certainly also 'Pop-Elektron' and 'Génération 80' on Belgian tv and the famous 'Rockpalast' on German WDR, a fantastic concert programme, where almost all the bands I like perform at least once. They always show a full hour of a live gig, really great.

One month later, the Comsats return to the Netherlands for another, smaller-scale festival, this time within cycling distance from Delft, where I live. By now I have become friends with Ciska, a girl a few years younger than me, and I am taking her to the festival. It will be her first introduction to the Comsats. We are the only two of our group of friends who are there.

This is another great gig, now also with a number of songs from the new record, *Fiction*, which is about to be released. I urgently need more pocket money, I think, I love it all so much. At this festival we manage to bluff ourselves backstage, so that we can continue our personal acquaintance. It will be a memorable day, especially for Ciska, for whom this is a real baptism of fire. She looks at Andy with big eyes and falls head over heels for him. That's how things are when you're fifteen.

Only two months later, in October 1982, the band are back again, this time for a regular club tour. Counting our pocket money, from this announced tour we choose three gigs that are relatively nearby.

I already know the Trojan Horse and the Paradiso. Tivoli on the Oudegracht in Utrecht has just recently opened. I can still see the building in my mind: from the canal you walk through a long corridor to a door, at the very end on the right. When it opens, you go through a courtyard garden to the building next door, where the actual venue is. About five concerts after opening, all the plants in the garden have been trampled to death, so the garden is tiled over. Later a roof will be added and it will become one building together with the actual venue. What a great place this is. We like to come here often.

During this year the foundation is laid for our Comsat addiction and for our growing friendship with the band. We stand at the front at every gig, usually right in front of Andy's keyboards, admire Steve as he sings, laugh at what Kevin is wearing now, and end up in the dressing room every night. In Amsterdam we go for a drink with Andy and Mik for the first time. At the end of this tour, we're totally hooked.

On the cover of OOR magazine! Photo: Kees Tabak

A little white lie

(August 1982, from my diary again)
Nahna and Claire can't make it, so when Ciska rings to say she's back from her holiday, I take her to the Waterpop festival. According to the schedule, the Comsats don't play until ten, and the rest of the line-up is rubbish, so we don't go out until early evening.

Upon arrival in Wateringen we walk straight to the gate where the artist entrance is. I head for a young man at the gate and lie that a Comsat roadie has two backstage passes for me, but I don't see him anywhere, so what shall I do now? No one from the band is there yet, he says, but we can wait here until the band arrives. Wow, he believes me.

After a long time a small van arrives, driven by a roadie who doesn't immediately recognise me. Fortunately, I recognise him, so I stick my head through his open side window and explain that I'm a friend of Claire's, you know. This makes an impression and he is very friendly. The band car will be there soon, he promises.

The guy at the gate looks on with interest and immediately comes over to ask, 'So, what did he say?' He already feels so sympathetic towards us that he has decided to arrange two backstage passes for us himself. We walk with him to the person who is in charge of the guest list. On the way we pass the van which contains all the band's equipment and instruments, and I give the roadie a wave.

It's worked. We each get a pass.

We take a seat on a manhole cover next to the car path. The helpful young man at the gate says in an apologetic tone: 'I'm sorry, but unfortunately you're not allowed on stage with those passes', assuming that's what we normally do. I put on my stoic face. 'Well, I've seen them up close so many times, this one time doesn't matter. Thank you for your help.'

So we're sitting there and after a while the same roadie appears and sits down next to me. 'Chilly, isn't it?' How English, I think. But it is cold indeed, and he says that until now they have always been in the Netherlands with good weather. That it can also rain here is news to him. He doesn't like it.

We get talking about OOR magazine and he asks if I know whether OOR rang that morning. No idea what he means, but Ciska has brought her copy with the Comsats on the cover with her, and he flips through it. Too bad he can't read it, he says, so I offer to translate it. He thinks that's a bit crazy (all of it?), so I'm only allowed to translate the subheadings.

He still wonders if he ought to know me and asks if we've spoken before. Yes, just over a month ago. He looks guilty because he can't remember, so I put him out of his misery and admit it was just a single sentence.

Neither of us wears a watch, but it must be after nine when suddenly the band car drives by. On our side, Steve is in the front and Andy is in the back. I look up pleasantly surprised and Andy sees that and makes a 'don't I know you?' face.

We suspect that they will immediately have a look at the stage and indeed they arrive after a few minutes. It feels a bit weird going after them, but we have to do something, so I call Andy's name. 'Hello, do you remember me?' He is surly and uninterested. 'Yes, your face looks vaguely familiar.' End of the conversation.

I try another band member. Mik shakes my hand and immediately enquires after Claire. She's ill, I say, so she can't come, and Mik (not terribly concerned): 'Oh, is she?' He also asks 'where's Nahna?' Well, she had no money and 'that bloke who was with you', I send him away on holiday. This later turns out to be true. Then Mik says they're going inside, because he thinks it's too cold, and see you later.

Shit. I'm very disappointed, because Andy was openly cold and Mik wasn't thrilled either. So have I been so mistaken? Only years later do I realise it probably was because it was just before showtime. They are tense and have no time for chatter.

Lesson learned today: don't disturb the band just before they have to go on. The hour before a gig, and half an hour after, are moments that the band need for themselves.

'Fortunately, the crowd that was there stayed, despite the rain,' Andy says later. That rain looks worse on stage because of the lights than it is.

It turns out that today is Andy's birthday, and a request comes from the stage if we could please sing to the birthday boy. Steve is serious, I believe, about that sense of humour of his. Anyway, he's on a roll tonight.

The concert is very good and they play five songs from *Fiction*, which will be released next week. The songs sound very promising.

Well, now that we have two passes, we'd better use them. Because of the earlier reception, I am rather nervous. Ridiculous of course, who could be afraid of the Comsats? Also, I want to wish Andy a happy birthday, and I want to know whether Mik did receive my letter this time. We find the right trailer and go inside.

Now that trailer is tiny, so ignoring someone is impossible and we quickly make contact. I tell Mik that I now also own the second album and that I like it 'despite what everyone says' and he is happy about that. At Parkpop I had told him that I hadn't bought the album yet because everyone told me it was 'awful'. He responded with a sigh and said he had heard that before.

So now he is pleasantly surprised.

But *Sleep No More* really is a beautiful album, it just doesn't make you very cheerful. The music is heavy and serious, full of doom-and-gloom, and drags itself along. But it's also very atmospheric, with echoing drums and only sporadically some guitar. The singing voice sounds vulnerable, emotional and somewhat lost. Sometimes I hear smouldering ashes. Listening to the entire album in one go is rather emotionally draining.

Nevertheless, I am really captivated by the music. At home the two Comsat albums never leave my turntable and I am very much looking forward to the new album. According to Mik, it is more like the first record, with more air.

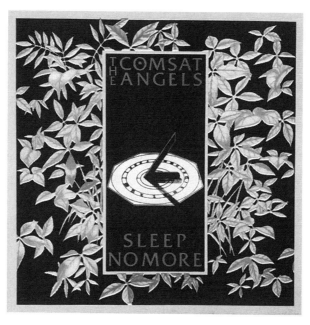

'Can you hear it whispering at the back of everything?'

The band move to the more spacious artist bar to have a drink and we go along. 'Hey Andy, cheers!' 'What for? Oh yes, my birthday.' He looks at his watch, it is 10 to 1, 'no, that was yesterday, or wait, it is now 10 to 12 in England, so it is still my birthday'.

Ciska and I linger at the bar while the Comsats move to the back of the room. Again I dare not approach them; I'm such a whimp!

We pretend that we are wrapped up in a highly interesting conversation, so that they won't think that we are waiting for them. Then it happens. Andy comes straight at us, hesitates and walks on, looks back, turns around and comes our way again. He begins to admire the trophy cabinet above my head, which he finds fascinating. Ha!

OK, if he takes the first step, I'll take the second. I ask him (how un-fanlike, sigh) when they think they'll be back. Andy takes the hint and sits down next to me, and will stay there for the next half hour.

We talk about all kinds of things, sometimes seriously, often silly, but always good fun. He says he never remembers names, only faces, and goes: 'Hello, you are… er…', makes a pensive face, thinks hard and looks a bit desperate, 'I don't remember', so for next time we know what we can expect.

I ask how it feels to be on the cover of OOR, well, great of course, only he is a bit sad that he can't read the text, but Steve was given translations of the large letters, so that's something.

Mik has joined us now. 'Hello, did you miss me?' 'Oh yes, Mik, I did.' Big smile. How nice this is. We were already having a lovely chat with Andy, but with Mik here it becomes even better.

I am wearing my Simple Minds badge and Andy leans over to see what it says: 'Nice badge, isn't that Promised you a miracle, parám pa pam pá', he begins to sing. Mik joins in and then sings more Simple Minds songs. Andy asks if I've already heard their new single. Not as good as 'parám pa pam pá, is it?' I'm now over my awe of him, and decide that Andy is actually really cute.

There is a bit of a teasing atmosphere, we're testing each other out. I say something to Mik at one point, but he is distracted and doesn't listen. So I say, mock-angry: 'Hey, I am talking to you!' He looks up and says 'Yes, I *know* you.' I ask Andy something, but someone else wants him too. He handles that, turns back to me and says, 'What did you say?' 'I don't remember,' I say, and he looks at the table with mostly-empty dishes next to him and raises his eyebrows at an unsuspecting piece of cheese, which doesn't offer a reply. By the way, where would that cheese come from? From France? I think it is from Switzerland and Andy says: 'They also speak French there'. Thus we babble on.

Mik raises a finger. 'Hey, I remember: aambeien!' So I say: 'very good!' Apparently Mik told Andy the story, because the English word isn't mentioned, but Andy knows exactly what we're talking about. He claims that it's bothering him at the moment and that it hurts a lot. But I'm getting the feeling that you can't always trust the pair of Mik and Andy together.

Mik has been away for a bit and now comes to say they have to go. OK Mik, and when do you think we can expect to see you again? He says it will probably be October, and starts listing where they are going: 'Amsterdam, Paradiso; The Hague, I mean, Den Haagggg; Utreggggt, Gggggroningen, Heendhoven, how do you pronounce that?' What? Oh, Eindhoven. Mik starts laughing, 'then I was right after all'. Did you have a bet? Well, Kevin knew for certain it was 'Eendhoven'. I laugh and explain that 'eend' means duck. Mik giggles, 'Duckhoven' and Andy tops him with 'Quackhoven'. What a pair.

Then they really leave. Mik gives me a rather limp hand. I turn up my nose and shake my hand a few times. He then gives me a kiss and whispers in my ear: 'my lips aren't as wet as my hands'. Well well!

Andy sees Mik kissing me and promptly doesn't shake Ciska's hand anymore, but kisses her on both cheeks, after which Ciska sort of faints. Then I also get kissed by Andy.

Steve is watching us and is having fun with what he sees. He keeps smiling. As he walks away, he gives me a wave, a little movie-star hand with his fingers back and forth. And that, while I never said a word to him. Nor to Kevin either, by the way, I didn't even say hello to him, I actually feel quite ashamed about that.

So I've decided that next time I'll head straight for Kevin, well, partially, because Mik and Andy (and Steve maybe?) shouldn't be neglected either.

OK, so they leave and five minutes later so do we. Phew, fortunately it's only a short time until October.

P.S. What is it with the postal services in England? Letter not received again. Andy teasing: 'Did you put enough stamps on it?' I have my address book with me, so I have Mik check it, but the address turns out to be correct. Now I don't understand at all!

Me in 1982. Simple Minds T-shirt and poster; on the wall three Comsat singles

Getting to know each other

Day 1, Utrecht, a bad start (October 1982)
At half past five a car drives up, and the band get out. Steve and Kevin don't recognise us, so they walk straight past us, Andy does recognise us of course, but he just looks at us from the corner of his eye and keeps walking. Mik does stop and shakes hands with Nahna and me, but doesn't seem to recognise Ciska. 'Hello Mik,' I say, 'we'd like to see the sound check. Can we come in with you?' 'No, you stay out here in the cold,' he says and enters the Tivoli. What?

In order to catch the last train, we have to leave no later than half past 11 and then we still have to run, so Ciska and I can't go to the dressing room after the gig. Nahna's train leaves twenty minutes after ours, so she can go in for a while. Andy asks her where Inge and Ciska have gone.

Ah, so saying nothing in the afternoon and walking by with a sour face doesn't automatically mean bad news.

Day 2, Amsterdam, sound check
We enter the Paradiso at the end of the afternoon and sit on our regular bench against the side wall, while the band are busy on stage. After a while, Andy climbs off the stage and comes towards us. He says hello to everyone and then goes to Nahna and says something, which I can't hear because Mik is making a lot of noise behind his drum kit. Andy then turns around and sits down next to me. Because of the noise we have to yell in each other's ear to understand anything.

An unknown girl comes in and sits down on the other side of him. In a quiet moment she says to Andy, in Dutch: 'Are you a Comsat?' Andy looks at me and raises his eyebrows.

After sound check, it's almost six o'clock, Mik and Andy are both sitting with us. They are going out for a drink and ask if we'd like to come along. Well, yes please, it's a so-called night concert tonight, so there's quite a bit of time to kill. So we all head off for a café close to the Paradiso and stay there until about nine. Mik, who is sitting next to me, starts to reminisce about his childhood. And when Mik relates something, he depicts things, so when someone is pushed in his story, I almost get pushed off my stool.

As we walk back to the Paradiso, Mik tells me his American adventures. The band did a short tour of the US and Canada this summer, and he mimics the American accent well. Andy hears him and immediately joins in. They're incredibly funny, both Mik and Andy, but when they combine forces, you really end up rolling on the floor with laughter. The comical Comsat duo, those two.

Guest list
After a fantastic gig we go down into the dungeons, where we are welcomed with open arms this time. I know the way by now. All my Paradiso gigs so far have involved me ending up in the dressing room, so it feels like safe and familiar territory.

Andy, who has by now realised that we are a bunch of fanatics, asks if we already have a ticket for 'It Pard van Troja' tomorrow. When we shake our heads, he immediately has Knarf, their manager, put us on the guest list.

Groupie
'If Claire hadn't brought them along last year, I wouldn't know these girls,' Andy explains to Knarf.
Knarf: Claire?
Andy: Yeah, you know, Jacqueline's friend.
Knarf: ???
Andy: Jacqueline, you know, Jackie?
Knarf: ???
Andy: Animal!

Now Knarf understands who Andy means. Jackie really is world famous in band land. Even this boring manager, who no groupie will ever want to seduce, knows her.

They're like ravens

Downstairs in the dressing room I ask Andy: 'What was the first encore again?' During the gig I was writing down the set list on a piece of paper, but because of the excitement in the audience, who kept clapping for another encore, I stopped writing. Why were there no set lists stuck onto the stage, as is usually the case?

'People always take them,' says Andy, 'and we want to reuse them.'

'Ah, that would probably be me, I always steal set lists,' I say. Andy has to chuckle. He's at the Paradiso, where they're always successful, so his day can't go wrong anyway.

Keyboard player Andy Peake, Paradiso 1982

The Trojan Horse poster, designer unknown. Mik is hoovering, Kevin looks at Andy playing, and Steve looks straight into the camera

Day 3, The Hague

The next afternoon Andy and us are upstairs in the foyer of the Trojan Horse. Kevin and Mik are already sound checking downstairs, Andy doesn't have to yet. We point out the gig poster for tonight, which hangs (hung, by now) in several places in the building. It is really lovely. The poster is one big black and white photo of the band, with red letters on it, beautifully designed. We just peeled three off the walls.

Andy wonders where we got those beautiful posters. When we tell him that, at risk of losing our lives, we have just pried them off some walls and rolled them up, he says: 'I should have known you would steal them'.

He actually would like to take one home himself, and coincidentally there is another one behind the bar. He can also reach it, but he doesn't dare to take it, being one of the band. Imagine the bar staff seeing it. That would be so *uncool*.

Too bad. No poster for Andy.

At the end of the evening, when everyone leaves and we go and wave goodbye to their car, we ourselves are waiting for my father's car. He's promised to come get us, but he hasn't arrived yet. 'Well, in an emergency you could always steal a bike,' says Andy.

On thin ice

There are now six of us, three band members, three girls, killing time after the sound check, upstairs at the Horse, when Kevin suddenly asks me if I've ever seen Simple Minds live. I'm known to like them very much.

Me: Of course, four times already.

Kevin: And did you meet them?

Me: Naturally.

Kevin: Oh, yes, naturally. And what are they like?

Me: Very nice.

Kevin: Like us, you mean.

Me: How do you think they are?

Kevin: Quiet. And weird.

Me: They're not weird at all, they're fun. There is one who is constantly making silly jokes.

Later I sit next to Mik, who apparently thinks he should also contribute. He says, 'That Jim Kerr, he's really ugly, isn't he?' His tone suggests I'm going to agree with him. I assume I have misunderstood, and stare at him with my mouth open.

Mik explains in great detail what's wrong with Jim Kerr: his eyes are too close together, he may be a singer but he looks more like a ballet dancer, and so on.

Excuse me? I finally come to my senses and start shouting at Mik with all my might. Where does this nonsense come from? Nahna and Ciska also catch on to what's happening – if anyone is very impressed by Jim Kerr, it's the three of us – and Mik is buried under an avalanche of insults. He crouches and looks around pitifully, as if he needs help. Is this jealousy, or what is this?

Whatever it is, it bothers him and he can't let it go, so moments later he attacks again. Last night they all listened to the mixtape I made for him, he says. And they jointly came up with a new title for a Simple Minds song: 'Promised you a song with the same notes'. All their songs are the same, according to him, and he demonstrates how to sing the same lyrics to all songs.

Come on, Mik, you don't need to be jealous. We really like your band very much, too. Honestly!

After the gig we are in the dressing room when Kevin mentions Simple Minds again. Mik immediately looks at me. 'I think it's better if we stop mentioning Simple Minds,' he says.

Finances
With Kevin we talk for a long time about how the band is doing financially. They are quite worried, because if the record sales don't improve soon, they may be forced to split up. Polydor, their record company, definitely thinks they are a good band, but had hoped for considerably higher sales figures. The Comsats fear that their contract

may not be renewed after the three albums they've made. It will later emerge that Polydor does indeed terminate the contract with the band one month later, and they have to look for a new deal. I'm already so involved with this band, I feel an icy shiver run down my spine at the words 'splitting up'.

Bass player Kevin Bacon, Paradiso 1982

Changing relationships
During the gig I suddenly become shy. Is it still OK to be in the front row? I don't know anymore. Now that I'm getting to know the band members better, it feels strange to keep up the old 'fan-band relationship', like during a gig. Them on stage, us on the floor. I feel like they are becoming friends of mine, not people to look up to.

After the gig they are completely exhausted and hang on a sofa like a bunch of living corpses. We're not much better off. I really don't understand how a band manages to do a multi-week tour. We're only doing three days and we're already worn out. There are no interesting conversations any more.

Saying goodbye

I'm still not quite sure what to make of Steve. At first I thought he might find it annoying that we always show up in their dressing room, but now I think he's fine with it, even though somehow he doesn't quite know how to join in. But he does seem to find it amusing to see how we interact with the rest of the band.

When saying goodbye at the stage door, we're all a bit hesitant. Should we kiss or not? Mik extends his arm to me and gives me another limp hand. He must be paying close attention to my face as he begins to apologise for his wet hands again. That's not the problem, I tell him, but that he gives me such a weak hand. Immediately the thumbscrews are tightened. I, in turn, squeeze very hard too, and Mik quickly withdraws his hand.

While all this is happening, Steve is chuckling to himself. He seems to find the whole thing funny. Not participating, but observing. What would he think of us?

Andy 'saves' the situation by saying: 'Don't look, I'm going to kiss them'. Everyone looks and smiles widely.

London

A month later Nahna and I go to London to see four different gigs in four days. Now that we are 'in the area', we visit the Comsat management, but Knarf himself isn't there. He happens to be in Sheffield for a meeting with the band, so that's bad luck. We leave a note for him in his office:

'Dear Frank, unfortunately we missed you when we came to see you. We hope the new material will turn out right. See you soon in Holland.

Love from Inge and Nahna, the two greatest Dutch Comsat fans.

P.S. Send our love to the band.'

Just before we're off to London, I send Andy a letter, but of course there is no reply. I didn't really expect one, but I certainly hoped.

What is it with these blokes, why don't they ever write back?

Just before Christmas we send Mik and Andy a card each, and a Christmas card actually comes back. And look at the date on the postmark: it was sent before we sent ours!

'The wind picks up the pieces, blows them all around'

On gig posters

Every venue employs someone who makes beautiful posters intended to lure people to a gig. The Paradiso's posters are famous. They hang outside on the façade, and inside near the stairs down to the toilets. I own a lot of Paradiso posters, and not just of Comsat gigs.

The Trojan Horse also regularly does very well. Tivoli in Utrecht sometimes also stands out, but in fact many venues try their best. They are almost never standard posters, where the band name and date are changed for each new gig, no, they are individual works of art.

Gig posters are generally A3 in size. This doesn't make them too big, and they are very easy to peel off a wall during an afternoon sound check (because they are usually attached with four drawing pins or with adhesive tape on the corners) and roll up. I always have a rubber band and a small roll of sticky tape in my bag for that very purpose.

After a gig, in the dressing room, a poster really is an ideal way to start a conversation with a band. 'Can you please sign my poster?' If you missed out this time, which sometimes happens, 'Would you sign my album sleeve, please?' will do as well. Of course this is only possible the first time you speak to a band. It would be extremely *uncool* to ask a band to sign something a second time. After the signing formality, the real conversation can begin.

Six Comsat posters are next to other in the hallway of my house. On that fine day in the nineties when the Comsats have no hotel due to a booking mistake, I take them back to my place, so that they at least have a roof over their heads... on that day Steve steps though my front door, a little unsure. He sees my hallway and all the Comsat posters hanging there side by side, and his eyes light up. If he ever had any doubts about me, they're now gone for ever.

Someone once described my house as a Comsat museum. Steve saw that too now. And it was good.

Paradiso posters 1981-1983, designed by Martin Kaye

Introductions

The story of the Comsats begins with Steve and Mik. The two come from a village near Sheffield and have known each other since primary school. In secondary school, they both teach themselves to play an instrument and join the school band, Steve as the guitarist and Mik as the drummer. After their final exams, one will go to Art School in Sheffield and the other will follow a catering course there.

At Art School, Steve meets Andy, who takes a number of the same classes. They start talking, discover a shared love of music and decide, second half of the seventies, to get a real band together. They need a drummer and a bass player, and Steve remembers his old schoolmate Mik. A 'bass player wanted' ad is placed in a local newspaper, which is read, purely by chance, by Kevin who does not live in Sheffield. Apparently, it had to be. Kevin writes a letter of application, does an audition and the band is complete.

In the early years the band has many different names and also switches musical styles a few times before they find the right one. They have to rehearse a lot, because they're not very good at first. This is also the reason for the various band names. If they have performed in a pub somewhere and it didn't go so well, the band is blacklisted and they are not allowed to play there again. With a new band name comes a new chance. In the end they decide to stay true to themselves, develop their own style, actually find a manager who believes in them, and The Comsat Angels are born.

Drummer Mik Glaisher

Mik is rather unique as a drummer. Other bands praise him and call him a shining example. When he drums he throws himself into battle with all his heart, yet his movements look smooth and graceful. No bashing around, no, Mik communicates with his drum kit and together they produce that characteristic sound. You immediately

Mik in the Paradiso dressing room, 1982

recognise Mik's drumming style. It sounds powerful and subtle at the same time. 'The man was born to drum,' I write after their reunion concert this century. It's an event I never expected, but dreamed about so badly. Fourteen years after they broke up, the Comsats together on stage again.

I owe my first real introduction to the whole backstage thing to Mik. Now that was fun! You have just watched someone play for an hour and a half, and a little later you are chatting to him for half an hour. I got all excited. If that first conversation with him had not gone so well, things might never have come this far with me and the Comsats.

Mik is a lovely man. He is emotional and incredibly witty. I don't always know what's going on in that head of his, but the result is often brilliant. He can even make jokes about his own career. 'We're the only band that started at the bottom and sank lower' is one of the first things I remember him saying. What was that, Mik?

I personally have always been very happy with Mik's choice of study, because, mamma mia, can he cook. Everything is delicious when Mik has been in the kitchen.

A pleasant, talkative man. For years he will suddenly shout 'aambeien!' through the dressing room. Mik can be very funny, as can Andy. But together they are just irresistible. After a gig we often go out with Mik and Andy. Tears run down my cheeks at times, sandwiched between England's funniest comedy duo.

Keyboard player Andy Peake

As a musician, he is the one who is 'classically trained'. That's how the rest of the band describe it. By this they mean that he used to have piano lessons for years and can read music. The rest of the band is self-taught. Andy's input into the music is sparse, but very effective. He rarely plays striking melodies or recurring tunes, he is instead the master of weird sounds, the accents in exactly the right places. His sense of timing is perfect.

At first he mainly plays on his synthesizers, but in the second half of the eighties he gets the chance to show his classical piano playing and he takes care of extensive piano intros or outros. The keyboard genius, the fans say. You hardly notice what his contribution to the music is, until you leave it out. He knows exactly how to give the music that suspenseful atmosphere, creating the unmistakable Comsat sound.

'Everyone fancies him, but I don't,' I write after that first meeting at the Horse. I changed my mind about that later. Not that he became my poster boy, but I was getting ever happier to see him. Andy is a very kind, polite, smart and witty man, who has great storytelling skills and a sublime ability to impersonate people. And he is also a great cook. What a band.

I still visit him at home regularly and our conversations are always interesting and open. I really like Andy.

Bass player Kevin Bacon

Kevin is a good bass player. The combination Kevin & Mik is widely praised as a very powerful rhythm section. They are well matched. Kev comes up with nice bass lines and with his instrument he sets the right tone. Especially during the time they are with record company Jive he manages to create a beat that is very danceable.

'Obviously a dull person with a very whimpy appearance'. That's how I describe him the very first time I see him play. Not much changed there over the years. Kev is a bit of a poser on stage, he stares dreamily at the ceiling, takes deep breaths, widens his nostrils, and really wears all the wrong clothes. His long blue tunic (Kevin's 'blue dress') is legendary, so uncool.

Andy still has the letter that Kevin, not yet 18 years old, wrote to the band in response to their ad. He is all bluff, but fortunately the band later on can see the funny side of that. 'Besides bass I also play, but do not possess, alto saxophone, cello, double bass (my first instrument) and guitar. I have had a fair amount of time on the road working almost every type of venue, including universities and gigs in and around London including the Marquee.' Yes, this is Kev all the way.

Singer and guitarist Stephen Fellows

Steve is a talented but not easy to understand person. He is very creative, has designed many of the record sleeves, and hears music in his head all the time. He writes all the lyrics and basically all melodies. He is brain and soul of the band.

During the early years three Comsats live in the same house in Sheffield, where they have a rehearsal room downstairs. Mik later says: 'Steve got an idea, went upstairs to work it out in his room, and when he finally came back down we knew there was new music. And it was almost always good. We filled things in with our own instruments, but the basic idea always came from Steve.'

The other band members always clearly put their own mark on all tracks. They also write things sometimes, but the initial melody or guitar tune and all the lyrics are Steve's. He is the linchpin of the band. No Steve, no Comsat Angels.

'Really nice to look at and nice to talk to,' I write in my diary after the Horse encounter. A remarkable first impression, I later think. Nice to look at, sure, but talk? Talk with Steve?

As a person, Steve is a bit distant, seems shy or uninterested in fans, and we're never quite sure what to make of him. After a few years we've come to know the other band members quite well, but what goes on in Steve's mind? Nevertheless, I always have a strong desire to have a real conversation with him one day. (It will take me four years.)

So we decide 'that you can't talk to Steve' and after a while hardly try anymore. We admire him on stage, and then see him in the dressing room, but there he usually keeps to himself.

Strangely enough, every now and then a fan steps into the dressing room, who then *does* talk to him. We conclude: if you don't know that you can't talk to Steve, then apparently you can.

The other band members don't always seem to understand him either and often find him difficult. A typical case of 'misunderstood genius', I think. Because there is no doubt in anyone's mind that Steve is a musical genius.

Manager Frank

Frank Silver is the band's manager. He looks like a real business man, neatly dressed, nice shirt, neat hair, moustache, glasses. He has an office in London, which is quite a distance from Sheffield, where the band live, so contact between manager and band is mainly by phone. He does regularly come along on tour, so we know him, too.

But make no mistake, this fine gentleman is very much a Comsat fan. He accidentally sees them play in the early days and the flame hits the pan. He immediately sees possibilities. They might go far, he thinks; the New Name-some-musical-greatness.

But despite being a huge fan, this manager is a real businessman in terms of behaviour. Listen to what the band wants? Don't be silly, money makes the world go round.

We, the fans, usually call him Knarf, which is Frank backwards. Ideal for gossiping about him while standing next to him.

Planning

When and where do they play, how do we get there, where do we sleep, who buys the tickets, and what time is the last train leaving? Following a band takes a lot of advance planning. We ring each other very often to discuss things. And we write each other many, many letters.

By now the composition of the group of friends with which we began this adventure has changed. Annemarie and Claire have disappeared from the scene, my new friend Caroline has been added. She occasionally comes along, just like Ronald. Nahna, Ciska and I remain the hard core.

For a while both Caroline and Nahna work as au pairs in London. As a result, they miss most of the Dutch gigs, but then they can catch those in London and the surrounding area. At that time Nahna is in regular contact with manager Knarf, who occasionally rings her when there is news.

From him Nahna hears noises, for instance, about an upcoming tour in the Netherlands, writes to me, and I rush to the magazine shop to find the details in the latest OOR.

When the band leaves for the ferry after a Dutch tour, we tell them that they can expect to see Nahna and Caroline at their gig in London next week. These are exciting times.

Caroline writes from London:
'I finally found the time to write to you. Not without reason, of course. I just heard on the radio that the Comsats, before they come to London, first go to Holland for five days. Well well, here they go again! It actually suits me fine, then you can warn them that I'm coming to see them in London. Let me know soon how the Comsat tour went and give my love to Ciska and the band.'

Caroline remembers:

'I went to see the Comsats a few times during my time in London. Nahna would come and stay with me. She'd bring a large jar of peanut butter and a knife to keep things as cheap as possible. She only had to buy bread every once in a while. That's what you two always did, she said, when you went to London together for a week of gigs.

One time we walked home after a Comsat gig somewhere in London, because public transport was no longer running. We walked through Hyde Park and then climbed on to Hampstead, where I lived. A long walk, which took us about two hours. We didn't think twice about that in those days. Andy thought we should have taken a taxi, but we decided that was too expensive.

When they played in Reading the next day, we had another problem, because once there it turned out that the last train left at 9 pm. This meant we would have had to leave before the gig even started. This was eventually solved by letting us ride back in the equipment van.

I wouldn't dream about doing something like that now, but at the time we thought it was totally normal. And quite doable. At that age you do everything without foreseeing the consequences. I often walked through London in the middle of the night, often by myself.'

To Ciska, who is on a family holiday in France, I write:

'Just received your letter this morning and it said if I could please say hello to Andy. Well, you can do that yourself now. If you come back on the 19th, you can go and see the Comsats on the 20th and 21st! Yes, you read that right. Yesterday I received a letter from Nahna and it said that Knarf had called, that the album was finished but not yet released, and that they were in Holland from 19-21 August, but of course I already knew that, she wrote. This was not the case, so it was a bit of a shock. By the way, I wonder if Andy hates celebrating his birthday with his family, because he always seems to be here for it. He probably enjoyed things last year, ha ha.'

To Nahna:

'Such adventures you're having with all those bands. And then those last casual sentences about the Comsats. No, I didn't know yet, what do you expect, I don't have a Knarf here.

Saw the new OOR today and the Comsats are in it for the 19th, in Eindhoven, but there is nothing for the 20th and 21st yet.

I got a bright idea and have asked Caroline if we can stay at hers on the 19th (because she actually lives in Eindhoven and she's coming back to the Netherlands for a short visit) and she said that's possible. Just. Incredibly, she travels from England on the night ferry and arrives exactly on the morning of the 19th. So she said she'd make coffee and then we and the Comsats are welcome.

(...)

Caroline tells me that the Eindhoven newspaper says that it's a multi-day festival, with art exhibitions and whatnot, and that on the Friday evening there will be a concert by a real celebrity, with three support acts, of which the Comsats are one. So it will be a very short gig and a kind of festival thing. So, no chance really to go to an afternoon sound check. They do, however, play at half past six, so if needs be we can still get home afterwards.'

Ciska from France:
'I have half and half agreed with my parents that we will all go to Paris together, and they will stay on for a few more days, and put me on the train home. Of course it sounds quite chic that I can tell the Comsats that I left Paris three days earlier especially to see them.

Are you buying the tickets? If so, please buy some for me too. And I don't know where they're playing (please not in Groningen), but if you're going to stay over somewhere, do arrange something for me as well. I think I'll get home Thursday night. Phone me, because maybe I'd like to join you on the 19th as well.

In case everything goes wrong in Paris, please write me a note, with all the Comsat dates and places and where you are, just to be sure.'

Note to Ciska:
'The 19th is extremely complicated and we were just so happy that everything was taken care of. Everything will go haywire if you're coming with us after all. We managed to get very cheap tickets

through Caroline's mum, who lives in Eindhoven, but if you buy one now, they are shockingly expensive, IF there are still tickets available, because there is a big celebrity playing that night.

Also, Caroline thinks that it's just Nahna and me coming to stay, and I can't reach her because she's still in London and won't be back until the morning of the 19th. In short: it's not really possible, sorry.

I did, however, come up with a money-saving idea for you, namely that you can buy a four day Teenager Train Tour. With it you can travel by train throughout the Netherlands for 40 guilders, so it is always cheaper.

P.S. I wonder what that extra guitarist the Comsats are bringing along will be like. His name is Paul, I believe.'

So, touring is quite a hassle, but still, we always manage, and the few times that we can't get back home, a solution always spontaneously falls out of the blue. Our guardian angels are doing their job well.

On topography

Where on earth is Heino?

The band have considerably more success on this side of the North Sea than at home in the UK. Now, the Netherlands has a reputation in this field anyway: we often recognise a good British band long before the British do.

So the Comsats play in the Netherlands very often; it becomes their second home. Some years they come in the spring, do a festival in the summer, and then another tour in the autumn. In 1983 they even tour here four times, in April, August, October and once again in December. That ferry just goes back and forth. Our friendship is growing nicely this way.

As big fans we try to get to as many gigs on every tour as money, school/study and other obligations allow. But not only does our relationship with the band grow with each gig, it also has another effect.

Every two weeks a new OOR comes out and we run to a shop to have a look at it, because it contains a list of upcoming gigs. When we read that the Comsats are coming over again, we run back home and dive into the old school atlas. Where the hell are some of these places?

As Westerners, as a rule we go to all gigs in Amsterdam, Utrecht, The Hague and Rotterdam. And with some regularity we take the train to Wageningen, Heiloo or Den Bosch. After a few years, the map of the Netherlands hardly holds any secrets anymore.

Noord-Scharwoude, Etten-Leur, Bergen op Zoom, Vlissingen, Uden, Vaals, Brummen, Baarlo, Lichtenvoorde, Heino – they were once just names, imaginary places, until the Comsats played there.

If only I was still in school, I would get an A for geography.

Motto: Get to know your own country – follow a band.

Vaals and Noord-Scharwoude

Vaals holds a special place in my heart. Situated in the extreme south of the country, the village is close to the 'three-country point'. Vaals, where I might never have gone to in my life, were it not for a gig by my favourite band. In Vaals there was a youth centre with the unusual name Spuugh (the Dutch word 'spuug' means spit, saliva). Yes, with an h. Why? No idea.

In Vaals there was also exactly one place to stay, Hotel Piet Haan, just outside the village on a motorway. Fortunately, it had its own bus stop.

Say 'Vaals' and I say 'Piet Haan'. We stayed there twice. The first time illegally, smuggled in by the extra guitarist who didn't want to leave us to our fate in the freezing cold. The trip there already cost so much, we really had no money left for a hotel, so he gave us his own bed and crawled under the blankets himself with one of the roadies. Eternal thanks, Paul.

The second time, three years later, we did pay for the privilege of sleeping there. Both times it was the middle of winter, snowing and freezing cold. Piet Haan was not very well insulated. This is an understatement.

Caroline remarked a year later: 'I'm sure the Comsats won't be coming any time soon, seeing it's a mild winter.'

At some point even Noord-Scharwoude and Etten-Leur started to sound less far away. You can get used to anything. But still, to go to a gig in Noord-Scharwoude, you take the train to Alkmaar, then a bus, and then it's a twenty-minute walk through the fields (unless you have a bicycle).

And yes, there is a venue there. Even in the middle of nowhere (my sincere apologies to the residents of N-S for this insult) you can go and see a gig.

In short, name a city/town/village/hamlet in the Netherlands, and if the Comsats ever played there, I will point it out. In my school atlas.

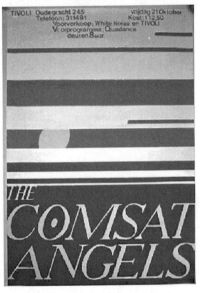

Posters for various venues, in various years,
and with thanks to the various designers

1983 – no fewer than four Dutch tours

The miracle happens. In January I receive a letter from Andy.

'Witness a rare event as I actually reply to a letter! Thanks very much for your Christmas/New year cards (also from Nahna), and your letter before that. I got the cards this morning; a nice surprise to prompt me into action. They are probably late due to the English postal system rather than anything else, but then that is no excuse for me to take two months to reply to a letter, is it? I've always been lazy.

You may or may not already know that we have parted company with Polydor now. As of the end of November in fact, and we are currently looking for a new contract. We are trying not to get too down about it all though, and as long as we find a new label soon, we should be alright, I think. It's just a question of finding the 'right' deal and hopefully getting back into the black, financially speaking.

At the moment we are writing and recording new songs, which we send to various interested record companies. For example, Frank has another appointment with one next week, so we're going to finish two songs in the next few days so he can play them to them.

The new stuff is, I think, a bit more commercial, or 'poppy' if you like, and we would like to have more songs in this vein. We are trying to get away from the 'gloomy' image we have, especially in England, but without totally changing the sound of the band of course.

We all really enjoyed our latest visit to Holland, it was one of the best ever. I think we shall be back quite soon; as soon as our house is in order.

Frank tells me you found his office in London. I hope he gave you a cup of coffee and wasn't too condescending!'

Audition
They do return soon, a few months later.

Especially the Paradiso gig on April 1st 1983 is something I have a vivid memory of. They blow the roof off. The band plays, leaves the stage, is clapped and shouted back by the audience, they play two encores, and go off again. The gig is over, the band thinks. The Paradiso staff think so too – the venue lights go on, music starts playing and we are expected to leave. But no. The crowd just keeps clapping and shouting and stamping loudly on the floor, hoping the band down in the dressing room will hear it. This takes one minute, five minutes, ten minutes. Clearly, the audience won't take no for an answer, *we want more*, much more.

After fifteen minutes the main lights are turned off, the music is switched off in the middle of a song and, oh yes, the band come back from the vaults for one more encore. What an unprecedented success.

And would you believe it, someone from record company Jive is in the enthusiastic audience tonight. He is obviously impressed and a new contract is in the works. What a huge relief for the band, but no less for us as concerned fans. This gig will later go down in history as the 'Jive audition'. Fortune seems to be smiling on the band, because this great gig in Amsterdam definitely helps them to a new record deal.

Kevin and Steve during the 'Jive-audition' at the Paradiso

After the concert we don't speak to the band, because they immediately leave for a business meeting with Jive. Make hay while the sun shines. We completely understand and are still jumping up and down ourselves. We do, however, leave a note at the reception of their hotel:

'A band that can do such a fantastic concert is bound to find a note at the hotel. We really hope Jive noticed there was something great going on, so that the deal was signed.

We're very sorry we can't make tonight and tomorrow. But we're definitely going to the Cattle Market Halls on Monday.

Anyway, 'break a leg' tonight and tomorrow (no, not two), we hope the cyclists make it on time.'

The latter is a reference to their gig in Noord-Scharwoude, which we would've liked to go to, but in the end decide against, because we really don't know how to get there, let alone get home from. None of us have a car yet.

The 'Cattle Market Halls', however, are doable. Another school-atlas place, and the place where we wait outside under two umbrellas for seven hours and are called 'groupies' several times.

'No,' we shout back, 'we work for TNO, we're testing umbrellas!'

New record

The album *Land* is released by Jive. A new beginning, but not really a new sound, fortunately. *Land* isn't that terribly different from the previous albums. However, the band now want to get rid of their gloomy image forever. Everything sounds a bit lighter. The music also becomes a lot more swinging. During gigs you really notice how danceable the new songs are.

I've always loved Steve's voice. He has a somewhat high voice and his singing is clear. On this new record he sings even better than before, and there is something warm and emotional to it. Of course he's also the one who writes all those beautiful lyrics, so he obviously feels something when he sings them. They're about something real, they're never your average 'the sky is blue and I love you' songs. There are more lyrical gems on this new album.

'Give it a name but don't colour it blue'

I sometimes notice that subconsciously I am quoting the lyrics. Someone says to me 'how lovely, the way you put that', and then I think for a moment 'oh, what did I say?' and soon after I realise it's part of a Comsat lyric.

Even today, I occasionally catch myself quoting Steve. That's what 40 years of singing along does to a person. A form of voluntary brainwashing.

And like a ship out on the ocean
Like the waves over the sea
Like the heat when the door is wide open
Sometimes I just wish we could be carried away

The new record also makes me view Kevin with a different eye. He puts down super nice basslines. Feet off the floor! Dancing at a Comsat gig is a new thing, but it makes me very happy. There is a radio recording of a concert at the Arena in Rotterdam, where you hear

Steve announce a very danceable *Land* song, followed by a totally recognisable scream from Ciska and me. How we dance this tour!

No diary this year

Unfortunately I am not writing in my diary this year, so I can't tell you any extensive stories. However, ever since my first gig (Herman Brood, 1978) I have been keeping a so-called Concert Booklet. For 45 years now, after every gig I write down a few key words about what was played and some details about the evening. About the three tours in August, October and December I find the following remarks.

August

Eindhoven: did not meet, just saw gig, but still a special event. Additional guitarist, Paul. As a result, Steve can do his best to finally become a 'groovy pop star'.

Uden: Steve smiles and waves during gig (!) and really becomes a star. Andy's birthday starts at midnight.

Heiloo: Andy is a big boy of 28 now! We give him a strange booklet with Dutch sentences such as 'can I get my hair cut here?'

Andy's birthday in Heiloo: me, Andy, Mik, Paul, unknown, Ciska, Nahna

October

Amsterdam: Mik really ought to become a stand-up comedian. 'Vinyl' magazines and photos are being stolen from us.

Utrecht: Kevin doesn't know us very well, he says, he thinks we are more 'Andy's region'. They won't be back until next summer, yuck! And I hate train strikes!

Rotterdam: an actual Comsat T-shirt! Kevin tells us about plectrums and fingers. Even worse than yesterday: they won't be back until December next year! Dressing room is full of groupies.

December

Vaals: Simple Minds' honour restored! Christmas presents (fez and Picasso) in bar after gig. All girls sleep together in one big bed (in Paul's room). Andy is jealous because I sent a letter to Mik instead of to him.

Amsterdam: Knarf is scraping car windows! Off to a club and afterwards a quiet party with Mik and Andy in their hotel room. Andy is super cute and Mik is super funny.

Den Bosch: Andy promises to send a picture of his cats, Paul will send us a Perfect Zebras poster. Ridiculously short farewell because of stupid hotel. Gig poster of an 'egg with a tuft on its head'.

Some of these notes I no longer understand myself. Other things made a big impression, such as travelling to Vaals. Trains and buses, lots of snow and nowhere to stay. Lots of fun amongst ourselves though. We see the band regularly, and we girls travel together a lot. It sometimes feels like one continuous school trip.

A resolution

Saying goodbye to the band is never a sad thing, because by now we fully trust they will be back soon. We never get to say to goodbye to Steve. He's always the first to go and sit in the car, trying to be invisible. We don't know any better and we no longer expect anything from him. So we almost fall over in surprise when on the first day of a new tour he says 'hello' first.

We've got used to his evasive behaviour, and in a way it also makes him rather fascinating. It's certainly made me *very* determined. One day, one day, one day I'm going to have an actual conversation with Steve, I promise myself.

It won't be next year though, because then they do only one single gig in the Netherlands. Bloody hell, wha's dis?

Andy and Ciska in a Vaals café, December 1983

Designer unknown, photo: Roy Tee

Business affairs

What the higher powers want

Record company Polydor gives the band all the space they need to do what they want. The music sounds the way they intend it, and the result is impressive. The music is sparse, original and honest, and the lyrics are beautiful, dark and a bit paranoid. 'That was the real Comsat sound', many people later say about the first three albums.

When they end up at Jive, a new, trendy record company, they lose some of that freedom. The producer Jive chooses even partly determines the music. Drummer Mik, for example, is replaced during the recordings by the newly invented and oh-so-trendy drum machine. The music no longer sounds sparse and sober, it is fuller and more like the trends of the time. Hopefully a bit more commercial, as Andy writes.

There are only four Comsats!

The fuller sound of the Jive era also leads to an extra guitarist going on tour with them in order to reproduce the album sound live. Three different guitarists succeed each other. They only last one year each and then disappear.

1983 – Paul, a pleasant, spontaneous guy, who also has his own band, Perfect Zebras. The year before he is hired to tour with the Comsats, the Perfect Zebras are their support act night after night, and there they discover his guitar skills. The Comsats travel to the Netherlands several times in his year, so we see Paul often. A few years after his departure, he suddenly takes part in the Eurovision Song Contest in some vague band. Well, I'll be!

1984 – In the year that Mick, guitarist number two, comes along, the Netherlands gets just one gig. I barely have a memory of him.

1985 – Ian, number three, is a bit shy. He is there during a long

Dutch tour, of which I attend eight gigs. Like the band, he also lives in Sheffield.

After these three attempts, the band give up. Apparently they can't find anyone they can put up with for longer than a year. When I cheekily suggest whether it wouldn't be better to find a fifth band member instead of a new temporary extra guitarist, Mik indignantly exclaims: 'No! There are only four Comsats! Only we understand how it's done!'

A few years later, when they make the switch to their third record company, Island Records (something which is achieved with the help of fellow musician Robert Palmer, who is a great Comsat fan and who recommends them to the boss of Island), the band regains considerably more control over the creative process. The music once again becomes a little 'emptier' and sounds less commercial again.

Communication Satellite Inc.
Without us in Europe noticing it, in America there are problems with the band name. There is an American company called *Communication Satellite Inc.*, in short 'Com Sat'. This company is not at all OK with the fact that an English band misuses 'their' name and threatens with a court case if this is not resolved. The record company therefore decides to change the band name on American releases. 'The Comsat

Angels' becomes 'The C.S. Angels' in America, and that's also how it is printed on all record sleeves and vinyl labels. On one album sleeve the letters 'om' and 'at' are even emphatically crossed out.

This goes well for a while. But then suddenly it's a problem again. And now for real. At the end of the eighties the Comsats can't use their name anymore at all, not even in Europe. In their Island years two albums come out, the first as The Comsat Angels (and C.S. Angels in America), the second as Dream Command. The old name has disappeared completely, and the new band name is now also used on this side of the world. But of course no one's ever heard of Dream Command.

When in the nineties they rise from their ashes after several years of having disappeared from the scene, the band simply calls itself The Comsat Angels again. Good thing, too.

Note: the band name does in fact stem from the brain of science-fiction writer J.G. Ballard. Steve Fellows once read a short story Ballard published in 1968, called 'The Comsat Angels', and thought it sounded good. No idea of course that one day there would be a communication satellite company who had thoughts about it. Things can go really strange. By the way, the contents of the short story have nothing to do with the band.

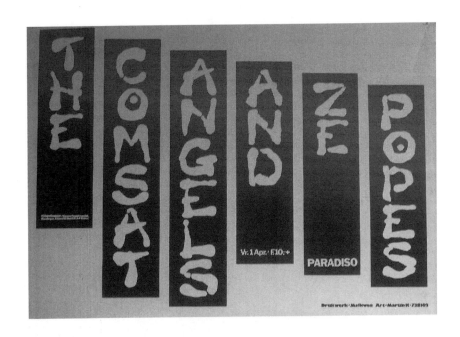

Designer: Martin Kaye

Fan club

For some time now we have been talking about the idea of starting a fan club for the Comsats. After all, this is the pre-Internet era, in which it is often difficult to obtain information. Googling when the new album will be released is not an option, and if your local record shop doesn't know either, then that's it.

The music world therefore relies heavily on fan clubs. We are members of a few ourselves. Several times a year you will receive a magazine with all kinds of news in it, with interviews with band members and photos, tour plans and reviews. And if a band doesn't have enough fans to justify the expense of a fan-club magazine, as an alternative there's the newsletter. You send a number of self-addressed envelopes with stamps on them to a management address, and as soon as there is something to report, an envelope with your own handwriting on it drops on the mat. Aha, a new album is coming, and hurrah, in two months the band will go on tour again. And apparently the bass player doesn't like Brussels sprouts, we now know.

In the summer of 1983 Ciska says: 'If I look forward to anything, it's the Comsats. So much so that I've explored the fan-club idea again and, if I may say so myself, I have quite a few good ideas. And next year I would have the time for it. So maybe we can make some tentative enquiries. I saw that there's a fan club which includes a letter from someone in the band with every magazine. Good idea.'

I write Mik a letter to discuss the plan. And then I can also take the sting out of the continuing pain point Simple Minds, once and for all.

'I've decided that it is about high time I make something really clear to you. Ciska told me that at the party in Zwolle (when I was at home, sob!) someone proposed having a questionnaire about what everybody in the room thought was the best band. And that the general opinion was that it would turn out to be U2 and Simple Minds. Well, somehow we still don't seem to be able to make you understand that we're not that interested in Simple Minds anymore. So I'll put it to you straight: <u>YOU</u>, yes, <u>the Comsats</u> are our favourite band!!

Will you please remember this? Will you please also stop all those frustrated remarks that all of you constantly make about Simple Minds? I know that you think this about us and Simple Minds because we talked a lot about them to you, but it never seems to have entered your head that we also talk *about you* to other bands. We're just chattering people, who talk about what they love, we can't help it!

For example, the band Sad Lovers and Giants (I think I mentioned that name to you once), well, they are very aware that Nahna and I are 'Comsat crazy'. In August they did a Dutch tour in exactly the same week you were over here, and we 'deserted' them after one single gig because we wanted to see you more. They didn't like it, believe me.

Well, you 'being the one and only' is finally off my chest, what a relief. And… I am not just writing this for no reason. This mouse has a tail, as the Dutch expression says. Here's the thing: after months of thinking and discussing, we've decided to suggest to you that if you are OK with it, we'd like to start a Comsat fan club. We already have a lot of ideas, but first we need your approval. So can you discuss it with the rest of the band? Whether you want a fan club at all, and whether you think we are the right people to start one.

I hope this is not too unexpected, because we have been thinking about this for a long time. We were a little worried that you might think fan clubs are stupid. Maybe you do. Well, please discuss it amongst yourselves and let me know what you think.'

Mik writes back:
'We've been talking a lot lately about the idea of a fan club in the Netherlands and we came to the conclusion that it would make more sense to wait a while until (if) we become more widely known in Holland. Then a fan club would be more useful to the group. Also we

could afford to have more photos and more merchandise etc.

So, if that happens we could then discuss the possibility of a fan club. We never seemed to have time to discuss it last time we were over there. Things seem to be more busy these days on the road if you know what I mean. It just seems harder to talk to people for very long nowadays – one entertains everybody collectively rather than talk to individuals privately. It's a funny relationship between people who entertain and people who are entertained. Both states of mind are opposites. Who entertains the entertainers? The answer is Frank – although he doesn't know it.

Give my regards to Nahna, Ronald and Ciska. Until our next visit, look after yourselves. You're my favourite Dutch people (apart from Father Christmas).'

The fan club never materialises. But then, eventually, in the nineties, when the band enters its second phase, I begin one anyway. On my own. But that's fine. My home address is listed as a fan-club address in the CD booklet and I advertise during gigs. Slowly, ever more people want to become members. Four times a year I produce a fan-club magazine – just as I imagined it ten years earlier, with interviews, photos, CD reviews and tour reports, and bits written by the band. I'm proud of it.

My heart is big enough for two

After 1983, which was all about the Comsats, there is an unexpected break. In April 1984, the band play just one Dutch gig, and that's it. We don't see them reappear the entire rest of the year. Whoah, we're going into rehab.

But don't assume that this was a lost year, far from it. When I consult my Concert Booklet, I went to more concerts this year than ever before or since. To be precise, I saw 48 gigs this year (almost one a week), of which only one by the Comsats. So did we need to be pitied? No. Were we missing the Comsats? Yes, we were, but there were plenty of fun distractions.

In February of this year, Ciska and I accidentally stumble upon another band. We walk unsuspectingly through Delft town centre on a Saturday afternoon when we pass our small local youth centre De Eland. There's a mega-sized, mega-yellow poster hanging by the door, with a close-up photo of four nice-looking guys. They're called Europeans and they're playing here tonight. Interesting! We should definitely go and have a look.

We go into the nearest record shop and I buy a 12-inch single by them. There are three songs on it, so at least we will be familiar with some music tonight. The three songs are played continuously for the rest of the afternoon and then we're off to the gig. The venue isn't large and there are maybe eighty people present. We are of course at the front. It's very energetic music, and we dance all night long. It's a tiny stage, so the band doesn't have much room to move, but it creates a very intimate atmosphere. What a great band, and in our own town, where no one ever comes to play!

After the gig we are still catching our breath when a roadie comes

straight at us from the dressing room. The band has noticed us during the gig and ask if we would like to come backstage. This is the world upside down, we think, but of course we go with him.

Ooh, good-looking keyboard player, I think. Mmm, cute drummer, Ciska thinks. The band is charmed by those two super-happy-looking girls, and they totally captivate us. They are friendly and attentive, hand us each a drink and then give us the third degree. What did we think of the gig, had we heard of them before, do we have any of their records and would we be interested in coming to their gig tomorrow night? Then they will play at the Amsterdam Milky Way. If they can have our names, they'll put us on the guest list.

   We have already spoken to many bands, but this is a new phenomenon. These guys apparently have an innate PR talent, because they do everything right. We are given the phone number of their hotel in Amsterdam with instructions to call the next morning, so that we can meet up and do something fun together in the afternoon. What kind of dream band is this?

'One more thing,' I say, 'that song you played twice, first in the set, and then again as an encore, I really liked it, what's it called?'

'She noticed! You really listened!', the handsome keyboard player says in surprise. His name is also Steve. (Apparently I like the name, because all my favourite bands have a Steve in them. This later takes on such proportions that people sometimes tease me with 'hey, I've found another band for your Steve collection'.)

The next day there is a nice February sun in Amsterdam and it is quite warm, so no one from the band is at the hotel when we ring, but we decide to go to Amsterdam early anyway. We find the band outside on the Leidseplein, having a drink. We join them, first for a coffee in the open air, later we move inside and spend hours chatting and laughing at the bar. The gig that night seems even better than the night before and I get a feeling similar to what I feel for the Comsats: 'this is totally my band, not just for now, but for ever'.

In retrospect, this will be my 'Europeans year'. I see them a total of ten times this year, but never again in the Netherlands. This is the first band, for whom I regularly travel abroad. In the autumn of this year, for example, they play in Folkestone, on the south coast of England. The band says that if we get ourselves there by train, they can give us a lift back to London in their van. This is such a fun adventure that we do another tour week at the end of November, this time in Germany.

Such excitement at the gigs, such fun backstage, another ride in their van, and staying in the same hotel as the band. Finally, we go to London again in December, this time for three Europeans Christmas gigs. I really am in seventh heaven.

It's a great year. I love their music, the electricity of their gigs, and all the travel adventures and funny conversations in the tour van. I simply have not one but two favourite bands, I decide at the end of the year.

But apparently it was too much fun, and it wasn't to last. The following year they split up. Oh no! The fairy tale is over. Back to reality, to my studies, to normal life.

Looking back, I think this may possibly have been the most exciting year of my life.

Life is all sound checks and dressing rooms

The following year I drown my double sorrows (no more Europeans and still no Comsats on the horizon) by enjoying other good bands and festivals even more. Below is just an example, based on my diary.

The Damned in Rotterdam, September 1985

In the afternoon Ronald and I go to Rotterdam for the sound check at the Arena. This is a good-sized venue, slightly smaller than the Paradiso, perhaps the size of the Trojan Horse in The Hague. The Comsats have also had several successful nights in here. In the late eighties, the venue will be renamed Nighttown. But now it is still called Arena, located on the West-Kruiskade, a ten-minute walk from Central Station. 'Snackbar Arena' is located across the street; a golden combination.

Sound checks are actually quite boring and mainly consist of hanging around. This one, by English punk band The Damned, is no exception. The drummer beats one drum for fifteen minutes (pock-pock-pock), then another for fifteen minutes (boom-boom-boom), while the sound engineer tries to determine the best sound. More bass, less bass, more reverb, less reverb, the slides go up, the slides go down.

Then the bass player plays the same two bars forty times over, and then the singer says into the microphone, seventy times in a row: 'Testing testing, one, two, one, two, testing testing, one, two'. They are, as the word says, checking the sound.

When after an hour everything has been set up properly, the band play two or three songs together to hear if everything sounds right, sometimes something from their own repertoire, but often also something by another band, a classic, or something which they actually think is idiotic.

There is a reason why we always love to go to sound checks. When the soundman is busy with the drummer, the rest of the band wander aimlessly back and forth through the room, kicking a ball or standing at the pinball machine. They're often pleased to find something or someone to pass the time with, so they're more than happy to chat with fans sitting in a corner, listening. We never impose on them, but we regularly smile in their direction, and usually someone comes to chat. They also regularly offer to put us on the guest list. So it's not only exciting to meet the band like this, it's often lucrative too, because every ticket we don't have to buy is money for our next gig.

Today our two 'great friends' Esther and Linda are there as well. They are the two groupies that we encounter very often at a sound check or in a dressing room. They have already seduced quite a lot of people from 'our bands'. Usually they don't want to know us, but they have realised by now that we are not all after the same thing.

We get talking and stay together until sound check is over. Today it isn't boring at all. Linda is in fact pursued all afternoon in a very tenacious manner by Adrian Borland, singer of the English band The Sound. He has been staying in the Netherlands for a while and often goes to gigs here. Adrian is an earlier conquest of Linda, but she now wants to get rid of him. However, he is completely besotted with her and says he wants to marry her. He ignores us being there and keeps telling her how much he loves her. Several times they disappear together to the lobby to 'talk it out' and then they reappear one by one with red eyes.

It really is a very frustrating situation. But for Ronald and me it is fascinating to watch. Linda, the hunted one, and poor Adrian the singer, oh, so in love. How many songs for The Sound would he write about her, I wonder.

A few years later, Ciska and her boyfriend are on the ferry to England and coincidentally bump into Adrian and Linda on deck. They are on their way to London, because he wants to introduce her to his parents. Well well, Adrian, the real deal. Unfortunately, I never found out how it all ended.

More merriment. The two groupies are plotting revenge against Kevin Comsat. He has spread the rumour that he has contracted a venereal disease from Esther, but she claims she never went with him.

Anyway, it is decided to make a toupee go up and down above his already somewhat balding head with a fishing rod during the next Comsat concert. Ha, this I have to see.

By the way, Steve and Mik Comsat recently did an interview for SKY Channel. I happened to fall in the middle of it, but since everything on SKY is repeated several times, I was able to record it later. They both have very long hair now, which looked OK on Mik, after some getting used to, but on Steve it really didn't look good. Anyway, never mind.

The Damned occasionally walk by and glance at us. We glance back, but nothing else happens. We stay put and after sound check (they play U2's *I will follow* and *Sunday bloody Sunday*, and *She sells Sanctuary* by The Cult) they play table football. Esther and I tease each other about who will get Dave Vanian (she really wants him, I don't). But I'm ahead of her because I bump into him head-on as I come out of the toilets. Ha! Physical contact already.

When the band leaves the venue after sound check, we eat rather disgusting chips in the snack bar across the street.

The gig is really good. It's funny to see that all the old punks have dug up their former gear (ripped clothes, mohawks, safety pins, leather jackets with badges and graffiti) from the mothballs.

Dave Vanian is gorgeous and I really want to go backstage, but the last train is calling, so I can't.

Beautiful men at the Paradiso
The next day The Damned play in Amsterdam and I go to the Paradiso together with Nahna and an acquaintance of hers. He has dyed black, very nicely backcombed hair, eyeliner and eye shadow, is cheerful and chatty, he has no girlfriend and he likes me too. Ideal.

Instead of 15 to 20, as last night, here at the Paradiso there are about 200 to 300 punks who push each other across the room and dance very ferociously. They're thrashing their arms and legs about wildly, so it's a big problem to get to the front, stay there, and not get too many bruises and punches.

Anyway, Dave, the vampire lookalike, is even more perfect than yesterday. Today he wears trousers that are so tight you'd think he couldn't breathe. Above that a blouse with lots of ruffles and lace at the front, and wide lace edges at the cuffs. Over that a deep purple velvet waste coat, starting where the ruffles of his shirt end, and over that a long purple 'pirate captain's coat', tapering to the waist and then tapering wide down to his knees. And then the white face, and long, tight, swept-back black hair with a white lock, and beautiful eyes. Phew, wow!!

Afterwards we are having a bit of trouble going backstage, but in the end I talk to a roadie and he says: 'Go on then'. And then it turns out that we have forgotten how to make contact with a band we don't know yet.

We are downstairs, in the hallway, and the dressing room door is closed, which always makes things much harder. However, Rat Scabies, the drummer, walks up and I stupidly (how uncool!) ask him for his autograph and then ask some silly routine questions. He says, 'Would you like a drink?' and 'Do come along to the dressing room'. When we're been in there for two seconds (Rat actually tries to start a real conversation, but we DON'T KNOW ANYTHING to say, shit...), people are about to leave, so I quickly go up to Dave for an autograph. The look on his face I will never forget. A bit annoyed, 'what a stupid, pathetic girl, with her autograph', and at the same time with something like pity because he thinks I'm genuinely happy with a scribble on a piece of paper. (Later, when leafing through the tv guide at home, I find a phrase that describes it perfectly: 'pity-tempered contempt'.) If only he knew, I'd rather not have had that autograph at all.

Later I also get one from the bass player. Not half as embarrassing. Now the only one I haven't spoken to is Catweazle (that's not his name, but that's what he looks like), and during the gig I was thinking that he was probably the only one I could say something to. Oh well, you can't win 'em all, although I would have loved to have spoken to The Damned and certainly to Dave in a more normal way.

On 'uncool'

Not 'cool'

Nowadays, the word 'cool' is everywhere again, as if it never left. It didn't exist at all in the eighties. What an old-fashioned word. The Fonz, in the tv series Happy Days, set in the fifties, he was cool. But that was then and this was now. Cool was just as old-fashioned a word as 'groovy' or 'far out'. It really wouldn't do. A very important new word though was 'uncool'.

In a time when being 'cool' meant nothing, you did have to be very careful not to come across as uncool. We 'wavers' of the eighties declared anything and everything uncool. People could look uncool (anyone who wasn't a waver was uncool anyway, so you didn't even need to think about that), but someone's behaviour could also be uncool. And that was almost a mortal sin.

Colours

We 'black people' of the eighties have rigid rules about appearance. In terms of clothing, in addition to black you can wear red, white or grey (if you have to, occasionally), but preferably not too often. Something small too, a scarf or your mittens. Other colours, forget it. Yellow, brown, orange, pink, green? Do you mind!

Hair

The most striking thing about us, besides all the black clothes, ear-rings, scarves and belts, is of course our hair. Gel, hair spray and backcombing are the keywords. First you put a lot of gel in your hair, because it makes it nice and sticky. Then you stand in front of the mirror for a long time with your comb, and comb your hair in the opposite direction, bit by bit. That doesn't immediately go well the first time, but you gradually get the hang of it. Our aim is to get the highest, the widest hair. I have a harder time than my friends because

Nahna on the train to Vaals, January 1987, never uncool

my hair is curly. You can do anything with straight hair, but curly hair won't be forced and does what it wants. But I try my best.

After about twenty minutes of backcombing, everything on your head is now standing up. So now you hang upside down with your can of hairspray (extra forte) in your hand. Spray, spray and spray again. All around your head, and then again just to be sure. Stand up straight to see the result, comb some hair back a little extra, and spray again.

Bands, audience, staff, everyone backcombs their hair. High, higher, the highest. The poisonous smell in the toilets of the venues and clubs is unbearable. But well, if you want to be beautiful, you have to suffer, as the Dutch expression says.

It also costs a fortune, all this hairspray. So, for the teenager with pocket money and the student with no income, there is also 'the poor man's alternative': sugar water. Putting sugar water in your hair and then letting it dry while you backcomb it is also a possibility. Sugar water is especially popular with those people who create punky spikes on their heads. It works well, but be really careful not to bump into anything, because such a spike can break off, and then you have lost a tuft of hair. Also watch out in winter, with hair that freezes. Same risk.

Behaviour

Try to look a bit arrogant, bored and not too interested. This is good. Being too enthusiastic, laughing too widely or participating with 'the plebs', no, uncool. Getting caught with pink-leg-warmer people, very bad; hanging out with other wavers and with the right bands, good.

You can't go to normal discos, because they are full of uncool people, and the chart music that is played is also not OK, so we have our own new-wave discos, later renamed clubs.

Before the Dutch night train is introduced in the mid-eighties, we often have time to kill in Amsterdam until the first train leaves at 5.30 am. We often go to the Mazzo or the Fizz. Everyone there is properly dressed, with the right hair and the correct facial expression, and dances to the right music. Often that is music by the band we just saw at the Paradiso.

We dance a little bent over, looking at the floor, which in English is called shoegazing, and in Dutch 'searching for pennies'. Not an uncool person to be seen for miles. How wonderful, a glass of berries in hand, watching well-dressed people like yourself.

Almost a day job
It's not easy, it is hard work. But if you're wearing the right clothes and your hair is looking good, if you have your bored face on and you look pityingly at people who wear a very uncool yellow T-shirt and enthusiastically discuss Modern Talking's new single, then you *are* part of the scene. And that is worth a lot.

P.S. Modern Talking is without a doubt the worst duo of the eighties. It is simply not possible to be more uncool than they are.

An authentic can of hairspray from 1984

Pandora's Music Box

The new-wave community annually comes together at the fantastic two-day Pandora's Music Box festival, which is organised three years in a row for 'our kind' at De Doelen in Rotterdam. Everyone who is anyone is there.

(From my unsurpassed diary, October 1985)
Managed to get to Pandora last Saturday after all. I actually found a ticket within five minutes and for the regular price. Pandora is something you really can't miss; you'd go there even when nothing interesting was playing, just to people watch and be able to say, 'Yeah, I've been to Pandora!' Moreover, I've been there every year so far.

I went with Ciska and Mathijs, who had drawn really overwhelmingly fat lines under his eyes. There were, of course, several 'phenomena' again, such as lady firefighters with projectiles, and a real oracle. There was also a girl in a bathing suit who stood in an aquarium filled with green lemonade, of which you could get a glass for free.

Everyone who entered was photographed. You had to be, it was a condition for being allowed to enter, and if you didn't want to, you got your money back. It is not yet known what will be done with the photos.

I was looking my eyes out at all the beautiful people again. Three or four times I saw someone, of whom I thought 'no, not very special' and that is an incredibly low number, I think. But the strange thing about a festival like Pandora is that as a festival-goer you start to shift your boundaries. At first you think: 'Wow, everyone is in black'. But you get used to that very quickly, and after a while the people who are just in black with backcombed hair aren't special anymore. I mean, on the street you would look at them with enthusiasm (not too much enthusiasm, that's uncool) as 'hurrah, a fellow waver', but at Pandora they are almost too commonplace. The same can be said about me, I have to admit.

Here at Pandora, you'll find girls in lacy black wedding dresses and boys in 18th-century nobility costumes. By the way, there were only trendy people, I don't think I saw even one single punk. Well, of course there were no punk bands playing.

At L'Attentat I bumped into Michel. That's a guy I know through Claire, when I spent more or less my entire summer at hers once. That is, I often stayed with her on weekends and on Fridays we went out to a new-wave club in Haarlem called Stalker, and I saw him there quite regularly. And he actually recognised me too, only, when I asked him if he remembered me, he said he had seen me, he thought, once. At least five times, I corrected him, but he looked unconvinced.

Nico was actually quite annoying. But she did sing, unaccompanied, *All Tomorrow's Parties* (which I know from Japan) and that was good. At The Long Ryders I almost passed out because I felt quite sick and it was really choking, so hot. After throwing up in the toilet and sitting in the hallway in a breeze, I felt better again, so we went to see Anne Clark. She played in the main hall and there we discovered the joys of sitting in a seat while watching a gig. There is something about that, although it shouldn't be a regular thing, of course, but just this once...

On to The Cult, because that's who I really came to see, besides Echo and the Bunnymen. Managed to get to the front, but right next to a speaker. And since even Ian isn't perfect if you can't see him (just the tip of his hat every now and then), and if you also have to stand with a finger in one ear the entire gig because of that speaker, then... Right, off to see Mac.

Ciska had left The Cult a little before me and so I was alone at Echo & B. It was really great, quite loud, but not so loud that I didn't almost drop off to sleep every now and then. How is it possible, nodding off at a loud Bunnymen gig? Rumours had circulated that they would first play their own work for an hour and then do Doors songs for another hour. 'But,' Mac said halfway, 'we only know two.' And so fortunately they stuck to their own songs. Especially during *The Killing Moon* and *Villiers Terrace* I was really swooning, and the songs followed each other in the set, too.

The unexpected hit was Nick Cave. Well, I did see The Birthday Party at the Horse in 1982 (very much so!), but still. I liked it then, but it was mostly a bloody racket, and that Nick Cave roared most of the time as well. But now, solo, it was really, really good. Of course it may have had something to do with the fact that it was from 3 to 4 am and we were almost asleep again, but I am seriously considering buying his latest album.

It has nothing to do with anything, but I would like to mention that he is far too thin, scarily so.

Over thirty years later
In the end, nothing is done with the mysterious mandatory visitor photos. Until they are suddenly found and released in 2017. Like stepping into a time machine. What a beautiful image of the 'underground scene' of the eighties. A sea of backcombed hair and black clothes. Entirely in Pandora style, the sudden find still causes quite a stir. The web site that has all the pictures is often difficult to reach.

In November 2017 Ciska happily posts on Facebook: 'The Pandora photos are also on Flickr! I've found us!'

In October 2018 Dig It Up, the 'treasure digger of Rotterdam cultural heritage', publishes a great article about the find on their web site (written by Dik Vuik):

Pandora's Music Box 1985 – Alternative pop music comes out of its shell
Post-punk, garage rock, industrial music, key figures from the sixties underground, a few commercial crowd pullers, performances, installations, presentations – it all comes together at Pandora's Music Box festival at De Doelen in Rotterdam.

My Pandora picture, taken by Mick Groot (Phoxx)

In the mid-eighties, the international alternative music scene is emerging from its shell and branching out in all sorts of directions. The greyness of punk's heyday (late seventies) is gradually making way for a more diverse and colourful zeitgeist. Post-punk bands that used to play in youth centres and basements are growing into larger venues and benefit from the emerging festival culture.

During its first edition in 1983 Pandora's Music Box brings a more alternative audience to De Doelen. The first edition of the two-day Pandora festival, and its follow-up, mainly attracts new wave enthusiasts. In addition to acts such as Siouxsie & the Banshees, Virgin Prunes, John Cale, Big Country and T.C. Matic, there are performances, readings and installations in the corridors: the 'plagues' of Pandora's box that tie in with the post-punk culture that already flirts with hell and damnation.

In 1985 Pandora attracts much more than alternativos dressed in dark outfits. A more colourfully dressed audience, from all over the country, is drawn to Nick Cave & The Bad Seeds, Nico & Band, The Cult, Alex Chilton, Fatal Flowers, Chris Isaak and many more. This has to do with the changing zeitgeist. The economic crisis of the late seventies and early eighties, the famous era of doom, is now really over. In addition, there is the growing prestige and commercial success of the festival: this time the 8,000 tickets sell out within one day.

By way of 'phenomenon' the organisers have devised this time that all visitors, including staff, must be photographed upon entry. The Rotterdam photographer Mick Groot (Phoxx) is hired for this big job.

Next to praise there are also critical sounds from the music press that Pandora is becoming too commercial. Internally, too, people realise that the festival is threatening to grow out of its shell, and the festival announces its own end. Nowadays it is clear that Pandora has played a pioneering role. Long before festivals such as Ein Abend in Wien, Lowlands and Motel Mozaïque, it offered a total experience with music, theatrical acts and presentations.

August 2019, Mojo exhibition

In Het Prinsenhof Museum in Delft I visit a retrospective exhibition about concert organiser Mojo. Part of the exhibition is dedicated to Pandora's Music Box. A card reads:

'In the first half of the '80s, the two-day alternative music festival Pandora's Music Box took place three times at De Doelen, Rotterdam. Enjoying music and alienating theatre. At the start a funeral procession. In between the bands a herd of sheep or a double of the royal family.'

In addition to posters, several objects are displayed. Like this card, which was handed to all visitors who had their photo taken:

'You were photographed entering De Doelen in Rotterdam on 11 or 12 October. This card serves as proof of this. Therefore keep it carefully. We advise you to fill in the right-hand column and send it in the enclosed envelope to our civil-law notary, Mr H. W. Heyman in Rotterdam.
Only if the negatives are printed will the envelopes be opened and will you receive further notice from the notary. If the negatives are not printed, the notary will destroy all unopened envelopes.
b.t.w. If you visit the festival on both evenings, you can simply walk through on Saturday evening on presentation of this card and you will no longer be photographed.'

There is also a handwritten A4 with a three-column list of possible acts for the first Pandora edition in 1983. The bands and acts are sorted by country. Some names are crossed out, others are highlighted in colour. It immediately becomes clear where most of the interesting bands come from: the list of acts from Great Britain is longer than all other categories combined.

My heart does a little jump when I see that the Comsats are listed as a possible act for the festival. Crossed out. Why? Was the band busy with those four Dutch tours or was there some other reason? Who can say?

As far as I'm concerned, Pandora was the best indoor festival ever. I went there every year. Amazing. After three successful editions, it was more or less replaced by the 'Ein Abend in Wien' festival. Also good, but just not quite…

Eight out of eleven

Summer 1985 (from diary number four)

At this moment I have been to exactly 140 gigs, of which only nine this year, which is a very small number compared to last year's 48. We last saw the Comsats 1,5 years ago for just one gig. Since then we have sent cards with birthdays and from holidays, but there is simply *no* response.

Nahna was in London last month and stopped by Knarf's office for the latest Comsat news. A new album is ready, *7 Day Weekend*, but it won't be released in Europe for the time being. No, first they're going to 'conquer America', and only when that job is done will they release it here. Oh, brilliant.

But now Nahna has read in the Melody Maker that they are going to play at a festival in London. What about America, we wondered, or is this performance supposed to be a try-out? We decided that we both felt like going to London, so if they don't go to America but do a tour in England soon, we'll go there.

Ciska and I were fantasizing the other day. Imagine the Comsats one day deciding to give up and coming over to do a farewell gig in Holland. How would that go? Will they cry (like we will) and will they finally understand how much they mean to us? We thought that three out of four would cry, but Andy wouldn't, or if he did, then alone in his hotel room.

Tonight Caroline rang. She'd seen the American (import) edition of *7 Day Weekend* in London, but it was 10 pounds, so she hadn't bought it.

OOR says

Ciska just phoned: the Comsats are coming at the end of November! And for no less than eleven gigs, and they do the tour that we used to dream of as the ideal (but impossible) tour. Five days close to home: Amsterdam, Haarlem, Utrecht, Rotterdam and The Hague. Also places like Noord-Scharwoude and Groningen, I believe, but well, don't think we'll make those. And the tour starts on the very day I'm due to hand in my final essay. After three pm that day, I'm pretty much a free woman!

I can hardly believe it. I had almost resigned myself to never seeing them again. And this year even! Hurrah!

'Just close your eyes and slip away with me'

Tivoli

Now how am I supposed to write all this down? So much has happened, everything good, and the Comsats seem to have missed us as much as we've missed them. Caroline was walking through Utrecht in the afternoon, when she happened to pass Hotel Smits and saw four bored Comsats sitting near the window. So she went in and had coffee with them for half an hour. Andy had quizzed her, she said, whether Ciska was still at school, and whether Nahna was working now, because she had been studying for such a long time. And how my studies were going, what year I was in. And he said that they had missed Holland so much and that they had looked forward to these weeks so much. And also that he got married. Caroline later told us in a strange way; she said that something had happened that we wouldn't like very much. So we almost panicked, but unnecessarily, because I think it's a nice bit of news.

So in the evening we went to the Tivoli with the whole gang. There was a support act that we didn't want to see, so we sat in the back and drank berries. Four to be exact and I was so tipsy (strong stuff, that) that I had trouble standing up. I hung onto Ciska to keep from falling over and I felt so overconfident that I could have walked into the dressing room there and then and told them how much I missed them.

Despite the fact that the whole fan base was complete and I knew there would be Comsats on stage, I couldn't quite imagine it. So when they came on it felt like I was dreaming. OK, I was also quite influenced by the four berries I drank, but I was afraid that if I opened my eyes they wouldn't be there anymore. Later that disappeared and I felt so happy and 'at home' again. Now I realised how much I've missed them in recent years. And yet it seemed so normal again, so familiar that they were standing there, as if they had never been gone.

During the third song or so Ciska and I (still leaning on each other) went to the front and suddenly Andy saw us and gave us a typical Andy look, I gave him a big smile and waved at him, and he smiled and waved back. All nerves were gone. I could legitimately go crazy.

Later in the dressing room, Andy asked us what we thought of the set. Were the new songs in the right place, or did we think things had to be switched around, because they hadn't figured that out yet. And after all, we were the experts, he said.

The gig itself went very well, everyone was dancing and clapping and very enthusiastic. Andy said they had been very worried if people would turn up.

Mik's hair is still very long, Caroline absolutely loves it. Fortunately Steve has had a haircut after that SKY interview in September.

Andy, November 1985

It was combed straight back from his face and he looked great.

Afterwards we were about to climb over the stage to go to the dressing room, but a rather pathetic young man sent us back, because the Comsats didn't want to see anyone afterwards, they had said.

I don't think he understood why we laughed in his face.

Perhaps it was because the berries had worn off again, but the first entrance into the dressing room was still a bit nerve-racking. Ciska and Caroline immediately threw themselves at Andy, and I headed straight for Mik. The conversation with Mik was a bit strange. Well, it was all about music, and that's never a good sign. I mean, we're supposed to talk about family and cats and strange food. But Mik was only saying things about the album and producers, and he wanted to know what I liked and didn't like about the new album, so I told him. But it went on and on, so after a while I tried to change the subject. But apparently he didn't want to, so I joined the Andy fan club.

Andy told stories about 'mean people' at Jive wanting to decide everything, and that the Comsats had no say in anything. As an example he mentioned shooting their latest video. 'That wasn't meant seriously, was it, those ridiculous synchronised dance steps,' I asked. Well, said Andy, the record company thought there should be a Motown-esque dance routine, and for that purpose they'd hired a real choreographer to prepare the band. Unfortunately, the choreographer had to leave after half an hour and the poor Comsats were left to themselves. They continued practising, outside in a square, with lots of children watching. 'It was so embarrassing,' said Andy. Not that embarrassing though, apparently, because he promptly started to show us the dance steps in the full dressing room.

There is a new guitarist again, Ian, and he didn't know what to make of it all. All those girls suddenly and everyone so excited, and apparently everyone knew each other well. I think he was a bit overwhelmed. He looked friendly, though, so one of these days I'm going to have a longer chat with him. When I asked him about Utrecht later, he said, 'I felt like I was at a party where I didn't know anyone.' Oh dear, the poor boy.

In some weird way I'm also a tiny bit disappointed, but it's not their fault and it's not ours. I think the problem is that I've finally completely lost the 'looking up to' feeling. This takes away a lot of frustration, but also many exciting jitters.

I think I was always a little in love before now. Not with a specific person in the band, but with the Band as an independent Something. In love with the person The Comsat Angels. But now we have passed the infatuation stage, sort of, the butterflies in my stomach have settled down, and we have now reached the 'love' phase. Something like that.

As much fun as it was last night, and just the way I've always wanted it to be, now and then I felt something like 'nothing spectacular is happening'. I used to have those infatuated feelings and actually that was really nice. At least it was such a big part of going to see the Comsats. The frustrations and the nerves and the hanging around made it all 'real'.

Now it was almost too relaxed. But I'm sure I'll get used to that quickly and it doesn't mean that I don't still want to go see them ten times this tour. Maybe it's what I said to Mik, who commented that we're 'suddenly smoking and drinking': we've grown up.

A short down moment

I'm tired already, after only two days. I arrived in The Hague yesterday in a bad mood. It hardly mattered that after a, I must admit, superb concert, the Comsats went straight from the dressing room into Knarf's car, without speaking to us. They muttered something about having to work and then they drove off. Andy opened the window for a second and called out to Ciska: 'which one is your little brother?' She pointed him out and Andy waved at him.

Cis is not going to Haarlem today, because her mother is throwing a party tonight. She has an exam on Monday, so she wasn't going to go to Zaandam tomorrow either. But she just rang to say she's changed her mind and wants to come after all. However, it is not at all certain that Zaandam in still in the plans. Anyway, I'm off to Haarlem now.

On my own, 3 pm

I'm sat in the station restaurant at Amsterdam Central and I don't know whether Nahna or Ciska or anyone will come tonight. The train to Zaandam will leave soon and I will be there at half past three. Then I need to find the venue and go to the sound check. If I get in at all, because in these smaller towns, that's often difficult.

What a strange evening yesterday in Haarlem! The gig was very good. Steve kept on making jokes on stage, even went down on his knees like a real rock star twice, and finally did a split jump in the air!

After the gig we waited too long, so when Nahna and I entered the dressing room they were just leaving. Mik came over to us and said that the one and only Robert Palmer had been in the audience and that they had an appointment with him at his hotel immediately. Wow.

7 pm
Gotta love these guys. They wrote the first verse of a 'rap' about Holland in the car this afternoon, and Kevin has just performed it on stage accompanied by drums.

I got here at four and I actually got in, and around six the band arrived. Andy came to sit with me and we chatted for half an hour, including me scolding him for never writing back. He admitted that he is ashamed of that. As soon as he gets home to Sheffield he'll send me a card. Yes, of course.

I told him Ciska and I are going on holiday to the UK next summer. He invited us to definitely come for tea when we are in Sheffield and that we really should let him know the exact dates.

Unbelievable but true: I've already said a couple of sentences to Steve twice now. He just took a picture of Kev, Andy, Ian and me together, and he's going to send me a copy, he promises.

I also finally talked to Ian; he is alright. I should not betray to the Comsats that he is so happy to play with them, because he has told me this 'in the strictest confidence'.

Frank is of course, as usual, pacing the room with his fingers in his ears like a shrewd businessman, looking at everything as critically as possible. Bah, I don't like that Knarf.

Just phoned Nahna, and she's coming after all. And could I please put her on the guest list!

Oh, and as for last night, the meeting with Robert Palmer. He is now in Milan, Andy writes in my concert booklet, but they had a good talk. He is a real fan of their music, and in March they might do something together. Not a whole album, Andy says, but they want to record something with him. Exciting!

Then sound check was over and Andy sat down next to me again. A moment later someone announced that food was ready in the dressing room, and Andy thought there was no point in my sitting alone, so I came along.

During the meal, Andy told me about Mick, the extra guitar player who came along in April last year. He'd lived above Kevin and had left with £100 in debt to Kevin, and he'd taken the vacuum cleaner too! Earlier, when I asked why Mick was gone, Andy said 'we asked him for one tour, but he thought it was forever'.

I suggested to Andy that maybe they should do a shorter tour next time. Because, I said, these four days have already cost me 125 guilders, to which Andy replied: 'You don't *have* to go to so many gigs'. 'Yes,' I said, 'I do. Even if I didn't want to, I'd just have to, but you probably don't know that feeling. I will never forgive myself if I don't go.' Andy smiled mysteriously, and said he actually understood me very well.

At one point a girl walked into the dressing room, who was the support act, and she started to lament that although the contract stated that she should start at 9.30 pm and the Comsats at 10 pm, she refused to go on when there were so few people in the venue yet. She was referred to Knarf to complain further.

After the gig, Kevin stood in the doorway of the dressing room with two bottles of white wine in his arms and said to me: 'You probably don't like wine, do you?' Yes, I do, I said, why? He gave me the bottles 'for tomorrow night'. And Mik said: 'The day after tomorrow, in Amsterdam, we should go out like we used to'. Well, we did just that.

Amsterdam

It was just too perfect in Amsterdam. After the gig, Nahna, Ciska, Caroline and I went out to a bar with Andy, Mik, Kev and Ian. We stayed there for hours and I finally said everything that has ever bothered me or that I ever wanted to ask.

Back to the beginning. Ciska and I went to the Paradiso together for the sound check, and we stood outside for about five minutes when Nahna and Ronald appeared. We all went in, and everyone but me was downstairs in the toilets when the Comsats came in. 'Are you alone again?' Andy asked, but that was not the case. Poor Andy, by the way, was sick with the flu, and not at all happy. The night before, in Groningen, his wallet had been stolen with his credit cards in it. He had no money at all.

The gig was excellent. Mik later said that he had seen me in the audience and that I seemed to be having a great time. This was true, but did he normally not see me? Yes I do, Mik said, because you're always standing in the same spot.

In the dressing room someone from the support act came in to ask if we had seen anything suspicious, because their bass had been stolen. Kevin got up to make sure his own bass was safe and immediately dropped it on my toes. Thanks. Andy came to stroke my foot a bit later in order to make it better.

It was really lovely, everyone sat in a circle, Andy and I shared a cigarette and a bag of crisps, and silly jokes kept flying through the dressing room.

Kevin then wanted to go out to a bar he knew. He couldn't remember what it was called, but it was 'next to the most famous sex shop in Amsterdam' on the Leidseplein. After Mik did a little dance with Ciska and asked me if my pearl necklace was real, which question Andy answered with 'yes, real nylon and real plastic', we set off for the café.

Now there was rain, snow, hail and sleet outside all at once, so I got my umbrella out and Andy came running to be under it as well. As he's taller than me, he held the umbrella and I held his arm, and thus we set off for the bar. Andy thought that umbrellas weren't really very useful, but that it was so cosy walking under one. And that he'd never owned one in his life. No way, I said, I have about twenty. Oh, said Andy, can I buy one from you? That was fine with me and he asked if I had a big black one and how much I wanted for it. Nice question for someone who has just had their wallet stolen. So I thought for a moment and said, 'I want to be on the guest list for the rest of the tour.' Well, that shouldn't be a problem.

The bar was quite full so we had to stand. Suddenly the opportunity presented itself to tell Andy about all our past frustrations. That we never dared to enter the dressing room, that we always said to each other 'no, you go' and tried to push each other in first. That we were often nervous about what mood they'd be in, etc. Andy could relate, because he'd been to dressing rooms himself and made the wrong comment, and was stared out of them. But, he said, it is very often not the band themselves, but the people around them who are annoying.

He told me of a time in England, when after a gig there were forty people in the hallway who wanted to talk to them, but a roadie wouldn't let them in. And that the Comsats thought: 'nobody wants to see us tonight, let's go home'. And then Kevin discovered all these people outside in the hallway and wanted to go to them. But the roadie had said, 'You can go out, but then you can't come back in!'

I went to the bar to get some drinks for Caroline and Andy. A few stools had become available, and Ian, Ciska and Mik were sitting at the bar. Mik asked 'his favourite Dutch girl' to join him and put his arm around my waist. I told him how happy I was that they were finally touring here again, that I'd been really afraid they would never show up again. His response was so sweet. He said that before he never understood 'how much the Comsats mean to you'. At first he thought it was just 'a bit of fun' for me, but that he had slowly but surely come to realise that it went much further than that. He went on to say that we were the ones he thought of when he thought of Holland. Also the country and the gigs, but primarily us. That he considered us really good friends. It made me very happy to hear that. He also remembered our very first conversation very well, he said.

In the meantime Andy was pulling my sleeve, 'where's my beer?' and so I tried to order again.

Then I talked to Andy about gossip. Whether they gossiped about us as much as we gossiped about them. Well, he didn't think so, or rather, they did gossip, but only about 'essential things'. Women gossiped very differently anyway, much more in detail, Andy thought. Because had he talked to Caroline in the afternoon in Utrecht, then in the evening everyone knew all the little unimportant details. Yes, but 'Caroline is such a gossip!', Andy and I decided in unison, while Caroline stood next to us, ha ha.

I closed the topic by saying 'We know a lot of things about you that you don't know that we know.' Andy smiled his mysterious smile again, but asked no further.

By now I was pretty tipsy and suddenly thought it was a super good idea to talk to my great friend Andy about my long-standing frustration. 'Shall I tell you something? I've wanted to talk to Steve for so long. But it never happens and it really annoys me.' Andy, who had had a few drinks himself, mainly thought that was funny. But he was flattered that I'd confided in him.

It later turned out that the very next day he had passed my confession on to Steve. I wasn't happy about this at first, but later I was, because from that moment on Steve said something to me every now and then.

Ciska really talked to Kevin for hours, I stole saté sticks from Ian, and the atmosphere was so friendly and relaxed that it really doesn't matter if the rest of the tour isn't as much fun, because I've had this now and no one can take it away from me.

And so this fantastic evening was followed by disaster, because that is how life works.

Wageningen

We were very tired ourselves, but didn't quite realise that they would be too. Especially because they had to get up much earlier than we did, as they had to be in Hilversum at noon to do a radio show. When in the afternoon, after ten trains and six buses, Ciska and I finally reached Wageningen and everyone just ignored us and it almost seemed as if they were angry with us, something broke and we just wanted to go home without seeing the gig. In the end we stayed.

Everything, really everything that could possibly go wrong during a gig, went wrong. First, a microphone fell off the drum stage. Then Kevin had to start a song but completely missed it, because his plectrum got hooked under a band-aid on his finger. It was at the beginning of the song and everyone was quiet, and then suddenly Kev exclaimed loudly through the venue: 'Shit!'

Then something was stuck in the drum kit, which Mik tried to unscrew with one hand, but it didn't work, and then he very angrily kicked half the drum kit off the stage. My heart stopped. He was so furious.

Then Steve got tangled up with the microphone cable and fell – thud – to the floor. And at the end of the gig, he threw his guitar on the stage and started jumping on it. And Andy! He looked so angry, so very angry!

So afterwards we'd lost all courage. I just wanted to go home. Ciska did want to go to the dressing room and Nahna, who had come after all in her mother's car, just wanted to stand in the hallway and be frustrated.

Last night we thought 'we've finally made it' and now we were back at two-years-ago level. Ciska set a good example and went into the dressing room by herself. Angry and aggressive? Not at all, they were in a great mood. Just Andy felt tired and a bit sick.

The entire band assumed that Rotterdam would be our last gig. We had to convince everyone in turn that we were going to Noord-Scharwoude as well.

On the way to Nahna's house we overtook their car. Knarf drove at a speed that suggested 'they were having a tea party,' Nahna said.

Rotterdam

Ciska and I went to the Arena around sound-check time, but we remained in the adjoining bar, as Music Box had come to film part of the sound check and to interview Mik and Steve. Andy and Ian came into the bar to get cigarettes, and a little later Mik came to say he was going to buy berries on the ferry. Then Andy came to get Mik because they had to leave and Mik broke off his story halfway through 'to sit in a boring hotel for four hours.'

John van Vueren, the tour organiser, also dropped by and got into a long chat with us. He said he planned to organise a big full-evening concert next year, with two sets of an hour, in which they could play both old and new songs. He also said that prior to this tour the Comsats had asked him if he thought we were going to show up. 'Well,' he had told them, 'I haven't heard from them in years. They always used to ring me before a tour.' This time we hadn't, so it remained a guess.

That evening was the best gig of the tour, I thought. The energy sparkled through the room.

The day after

They've gone home, and I miss them already... Last night was a really great end to the tour though. The venue was very full and the band was in a radiant mood.

Ciska and I had had a bet whether we would (me) or wouldn't (Ciska) be on the guest list. We weren't, so my first remark to Andy was that I wanted my umbrella back. Andy began to apologise profusely, the sweetheart, explaining that the tour manager had not been there in the afternoon, and there was no one else who could put us on the list. Mik later said he suddenly spotted us in the audience and had said to himself, 'Now we have something to play for'.

A few years ago they played in Noord-Scharwoude as well, but then we couldn't go because we didn't know how on earth to get there. Our excuse was that there was no train station and that the only way to get there was on a bicycle. And really, we hadn't even been in for ten minutes when there was an announcement: could all people who had come on their bicycles please look in their pockets, because a bicycle key had been found. Andy found it very funny and topped it by saying 'will the owner of such-and-such a tractor please come and move his horse'.

Andy asked us how we got here today, so I said: first we took a train, then a bus and then we walked for fifteen minutes through the fields and along industrial warehouses. And that was somewhat unnerving, because there were no houses or farms to be seen any-where, so we couldn't ask anyone for directions. 'How will you get back then?' Andy asked.

Afterwards in the dressing room I was sitting between Mik and Steve, and suddenly I saw the long-sought opportunity to strike up a con-versation. So I said to Steve, 'Now, for eight concerts I've heard you talk on stage about Robert Johnson, but I still don't quite understand who he is.' Steve was a bit reluctant at first and tried to put me off by saying 'try and find that out for yourself', but when I persisted, he went into great detail about who, what and where. He seemed quite surprised that I asked about it.

So, Robert Johnson was a blues musician from the twenties and thirties, who had been very original and innovative. He was poisoned and died at the age of 22, and there are no photographs of him in existence at all. But some music did survive?, I asked. Steve said that at the time there had been a radio station that recorded all kinds of performances, including Robert Johnson's. Steve had a few tapes at home himself. They were actually fairly easy to get hold of, he said, but he suspected I wouldn't like the music very much.

I asked Steve why exactly he mentioned him during their song *You Move me*, and he said that most of the lyrics in that song came from Robert Johnson, especially 'the train had two lights on behind, blue was my blues…' 'And red was my mind,' I finished his sentence. Steve looked surprised that I knew the lyrics by heart. He said that the whole song was in fact dedicated to Robert Johnson. I asked if the people of his time knew Robert Johnson at all, and Steve said he had died in complete obscurity. Oh dear, the stereotypical image of a great but misunderstood artist.

In fact, it wasn't so much a chat as a monologue on Steve's part, but its consequences are barely proportionate to the length and content of our conversation. I'll come back to that.

After this chat I looked at Andy and raised my eyebrows, 'did you see, did you see?' Andy gave me an overwhelming big smile and looked very encouraging and also a little endeared. Look at the girl, how happy she is now.

Some girls walked into the dressing room wanting autographs, and one approached Andy. She got her scribble and I said, 'Hm, no one ever wants my autograph.' 'Yes, they do,' Andy said, 'me, now!' So I looked at him in disbelief and he explained that the piece of paper with my new address had been in the wallet that was stolen in Groningen. Could I write it down for him again? And sign it this time, in his official tour itinerary?

'Can you read it?' I asked, and – these Comsats do pick up a few things from all that touring here – Andy started to read it out loud in faultless Dutch. He could even pronounce the post code and my telephone number correctly. Then he muttered something like 'oh, phone number, maybe I can... no, I won't make any promises I'm not sure I can keep'. And he started apologising in advance about how expensive phoning from the UK was. The idea! The phone's ringing, and it is Andy! It would scare me half to death.

At one point, a joint passed through the dressing room and Andy took it and passed it on to Mik. There was some serious doubting and finally it was handed to Ciska. When Ciska had the actual nerve to take a drag, Mik burst out: 'You stop paying attention to these girls for two years, and they drink, smoke, use drugs and get drunk!' It seemed as if he was really indignant. But we know Mik better than that, don't we?

People started to get up to leave. Kevin wanted to be reminded again of how we in Holland kiss people goodbye, didn't we have a special formula for that? Yes, it's always three kisses: 'left, right, front'. That 'front' caused enormous hilarity. Kevin immediately started practising on Ciska, because he has really discovered her since the café in Amsterdam. But well well, how subtle, he kept making mistakes in the kissing order and then it had to be done again. 'Left-right-left, no, wrong, again, right-left, wrong, I should have started with left' and so on, until he had given her at least twenty kisses.

Everyone started walking towards the exit. Suddenly Steve and I were standing there alone. With a meaningful look he said to me: 'You talked to me, didn't you?' and I thought 'oh shit, that Andy!' But it's good really, because Steve would normally have been outside in the car by now, and this time he kept making remarks.

He even started talking about extra guitarist Paul (the Comsats never gossip amongst themselves, it turns out again) and started explaining that they hadn't kicked him out, but that he had left. He said, 'You like Paul, don't you?' He suspected I thought it wasn't fair, and wanted to know if I was on Paul's side. I looked at him for a moment, then said 'no comment'. Steve said, 'I don't know what Paul has been saying to you all, but…' 'Paul hasn't said anything,' I said, 'this is my own idea' and that's the truth. Steve: 'But you don't know Paul like we know him.' So I said, 'Do you mind if I have my own opinion on that?' No no, of course not, said Steve, go ahead, go ahead!

Subject closed, I thought. But Ian came out and Steve put his arm around Ian's shoulders and said, 'Ian's such a nice guy, I think we'll keep him with us'. I will never forget the look on Ian's face.

We went out into the freezing cold again. Mik, Kevin, Ian, Nahna, and Ciska stayed behind for some reason, so Andy, Steve and I reached their car first.

Suddenly the farewell fell on top of me and I said, 'I don't want you to leave,' five times in a row. Steve apparently found that so touching that he took a step forward, hugged me and gave me a kiss. Steve! Someone I haven't exchanged more than three words with in four years' time, and now suddenly he's loosening up. On the last day, at the very last hour. I think he was startled himself, by the way, because he immediately took a step back.

But the best was yet to come. I cried again that I was going to miss them so much and Andy put an arm around me, gave me a cuddle and whispered something so very sweet in my ear.

Three days later

I can't stop thinking about Andy's remark. Not that I'm seeing pink elephants or anything, really, but he's been in my head all day. Last night I was at the Ahoy and I thought only about the Comsats, and halfway through I almost wanted to leave the gig and go home. But I thought I should give Simple Minds a chance, and I am glad I did, because I was quite into it for a while. Well, Simple Minds and the Comsats are unrelated really. And it's not a case of either/or.

At the end of the gig, the venue lights came on, everyone got up to leave, and then suddenly a Comsat song was heard through the speakers. Ciska and I both screamed and hugged each other, we were so emotional. The Comsats getting played in a venue for 8,000 people!

During the concert I was thinking about what Andy had been fantasizing about. If they were to play in a large hall or preferably a football stadium. That a ticket would cost 10 pounds and that we would be sitting 80 metres from the stage and couldn't see very much. I asked him: 'Do you think we'd still come?' 'Eh, no,' said Andy, 'but then we'll meet in the car park after the gig and have coffee together.'

So now that I was sitting here seeing Simple Minds, I started to wonder about if I would really go if I knew that I would be sitting where I was now. Seeing a Comsat gig from afar, no backstage pass and no real chance to speak to them. Don't know. It would most likely never be the case, because we *would* have a pass. Some things happened on this tour that cannot be reversed.

I meant what I said to Mik in Amsterdam: 'I don't want my bands to get too big'. In the case of Simple Minds it doesn't matter anymore, we lost them a long time ago, but imagine that the Comsats played three days in a row at the Ahoy. I don't think I'd like it.

Christmas

Yesterday Ciska and I made holiday plans for next summer again, and Sheffield is still on the itinerary. There is something called a BritRail

Pass, which you can use on all trains in Britain for three weeks, for 330 guilders. By the way, Ciska seems to think a 15 kilo rucksack is quite a normal thing! Well, I can't even get it off the ground, so she can carry the tent.

Today I started writing a letter to Andy. Amongst other things, I'm telling him about all the ghosts that always reappear after a tour, because afterwards everything always seems so different than at the time it happens.

In the latest Vinyl magazine there is a long article about Robert Johnson. I read it and was delighted to see Steve's name mentioned. By the way, it snowed all day today and it's snowing even now. Everything is white, there is really a thick layer. Nice to see, and I feel cosy and safe inside. Writing essays and letters, studying, I am sailing through it all. It should snow all year round.

On venues

'Maybe you could write something about youth centres,' Steve recently suggests when I tell him I'm working on this book and what topics I'm writing about. Why youth centres, I ask him, is that interesting? Or relevant?

Yes, says Steve, because there wasn't such a thing in England at the time at all. Youth centres were a typical Dutch phenomenon and we benefited greatly from them. One of the reasons we played in Holland so often was because of all these youth centres everywhere. Exactly the group of people we were aiming to reach.

All right, youth centres it is. I had never realised that they were unique to the Netherlands.

In the time this story is set the Netherlands had venues in various sizes. The really big names played in football stadiums, such as the Feyenoord Stadium in Rotterdam (the Stones for example, and David Bowie) or, somewhat smaller, at the Ahoy, which could accommodate about 8,000 music lovers. The large halls of today – the Ziggo Dome or AFAS Live – did not yet exist. A level below the Ahoy there were venues such as Muziekcentrum Vredenburg in Utrecht, De Doelen in Rotterdam, or Carré in Amsterdam.

My gig life usually took place in venues one level below all these, in the so-called 'club circuit'. We're talking about the smaller venues, where not yet famous or beginning bands play, with a capacity of between 500 and 1200 visitors.

In the eighties these were for example: Paradiso and Milky Way (Amsterdam), Tivoli and Vrije Vloer (Utrecht), Patronaat (Haarlem), Arena and Lantaren (Rotterdam), LVC (Leiden), Noorderligt (Tilburg), Vera (Groningen), Vereeniging (Nijmegen), Casino (Den Bosch) and Nieuwe Pul (Uden). This is the kind of venue where the Comsats usually played. Not too big and in an intimate setting.

But, Steve has a point – youth centres regularly organised gigs as well.

In the twentieth century, when there were still occasionally a few sensible politicians in government, youth centres were seen as an ideal way of keeping young people off the streets and to offer them their own place. And so, youth centres were subsidised by the government. Every town had at least one, and in the big cities usually every neighbourhood had one.

With the money they received all sorts of things were organised for adolescents and people in their twenties. They were meeting places, there was a bar, a pinball machine and a table-tennis table, and they also organised dance nights. Every week there were activities and you could learn a thing or two there as well. Anything to keep young people happy and off the streets.

And yes, as a rule they received enough money to be able to invite bands to come and play. In this respect, the youth centres were a good addition to the regular venues and clubs. I have seen many a great gig in a youth centre – in Buk Buk in Heiloo, Eland in Delft, Drieluik in Zaandam, De Koog in Noord-Scharwoude, or Spuugh in Vaals, to name but a few. Even the Trojan Horse in The Hague was originally a youth centre.

Youth centres were very popular and clearly fulfilled a need. In this century many of them were closed due to a lack of funding, like so many wonderful things that made life better. A very great shame.

P.S. Steve does forget though, that the UK has its own typical gig circuit that Holland has never known: colleges. Almost every British university has its own venue. The Comsats played these regularly as well. So every country has its own peculiarities, I am pleased to say.

First time in Sheffield

Anticipation

We make more and more concrete holiday plans and fantasize about what could happen when we're in Sheffield. Will we just see them over a cup of coffee or will we perhaps be invited for a meal? How would they behave in front of their wives and girl-friends, have they told them about us? Maybe we can see them rehearse.

Nahna has just been to London and brings bad news. She went to see Europeans' manager and what we already suspected turns out to be true. They broke up. Steve-2 and Colin now have a new band together, but under what name is still unknown.

The second piece of news comes from Knarf: in America the name Comsat Angels has always been a problem, and on tour there they were always called C.S. Angels. But now the name is completely forbidden, in Europe as well. So they have to find a new band name. Nahna was in Knarf's office and says that every three minutes he threw a possible name on the table, and could she please help and think of a suitable one. What if they come on tour? Then no one, including us, will know who they are.

On holiday!

The day finally comes. Ciska and I are going on that much-talked-about holiday to the United Kingdom. We want to start with a lot of walking, following the long-distance trail the Pennine Way. We have a heavy tent with us and cooking and sleeping gear, and head into the unknown. We would also like to go to Edinburgh because of the Fringe Festival, annually held in August, which has lots of small-scale plays and free street theatre.

We have an itinerary ready for the first weeks, which we intend to follow rigorously. How the days in Sheffield will go? That can really go every which way.

Our journey begins on August 1, 1986. We take the Budget Bus from The Hague with all our heavy luggage. This bus drives to Zeebrugge, embarks on the ferry, and on the other side drives on to London. From there we're going to take a National Express coach north to York, where we will stay for a few days and then continue on to Manchester. There the walking will begin.

Last May Ciska and I met two nice chaps during a gig at the Horse. And would you believe it, one of the two, Lex, happens to be on the very same bus. He is going to spend a week in London with another friend of his, Caspar.

Just yesterday I found out that Steve-2 and Colin's new band is called 'How we Live' and that they have a single out. I'm telling Ciska this piece of news on the bus, and apparently Lex and Caspar are listening in. When we arrive in London, the four of us go for a farewell coffee at Victoria Station. Lex is leafing through the Time Out he's just bought, comes across something interesting and reads in a teasing tone of voice: 'How we Live, tomorrow at the Marquee'.

Our coach ticket to York for in an hour has just been bought, so we can't go. Lex does not know what he's caused, because I'm going crazy. Steve and Colin from Europeans are playing in London tomorrow and I'm taking a coach to York? You don't really think so, do you!

It almost turns into a fight, because Ciska insists on sticking to the plan and not messing everything up 'for a band', and I just yell things like 'I want to go there!' and 'we could also do London at the beginning of the holiday rather than at the end'. But Ciska really wants to go to the countryside first. In the end I decide to give in, so as not to ruin the mood right at the start of the trip. But I really don't like it.

In any case, we think Lex and Caspar should go to the gig and say hello to Steve-2 for us. I want to write him a note, but there's no time for that. We board the bus to York.

For a week we walk part of the Pennine Way, walking from youth hostel to campsite, with me camping for the first time ever. We travel via Carlisle to Edinburgh for a few days of theatre festival. Everything turns out to be fully booked there, so we end up on a campsite well outside the city.

Below follows, again from my diary, how the journey goes after that.

Friday August 15, 1986
Today really is the lowest point of the holiday. There's pouring rain, we fight, and everything else goes wrong too. We have just booked a coach to Sheffield for Sunday. Shit, £9.50 per person. The bus leaves at 10.30 and doesn't get to Sheffield until 18.20, hallelujah.

We try hard all day to go to all kinds of plays, but it seems it's not to be. Deeply disillusioned back at the campsite. At night a terrible hurricane, wind force 300!

Saturday August 16
Rucksacks already packed at the campsite. Ciska tries to call Andy, but he's not at home. We hope he was just out and not still away on holiday.

Sunday August 17
Off to Sheffield! The plan is to leave for London on Tuesday afternoon, to spend the rest of our money there for two days, and to visit people such as extra guitarist Paul. But no, it all turns out completely different.

At half past six in the evening the National Express coach arrives at the bus station. It's Sunday, the tourist office is closed and we don't have a place to sleep yet. No one knows anything about bed and breakfasts, except for one that's in a faraway suburb. Well, better go there then.

At 9 pm we arrive at The Peace Guest House, which is a bit scary, because it has everything to do with some vague religion, of which leaflets are scattered everywhere.

Ciska tries to call Andy again, but he really isn't there. Then she calls Mik, who is completely lost for a moment because he wasn't expecting us. But we make an appointment to visit him tomorrow afternoon.

We go to the Pizza Hut and spot Phil Oakey of The Human League walking down the street.

Monday August 18

First off we go to the bus station to buy a coach ticket to London (15 pounds in all). Then to the Tourist Information (without rucksacks, we put them in a locker at the bus station for the time being) to find a new B&B. We get a list of B&Bs and choose one in Broomhill Street.

So, armed with a map, we set off, but there is no B&B in Broomhill Street. Strange, until we discover, and then we've been searching for about three hours, that there's a Broomhill Street and a Broomhall Street. Obviously we are in the wrong one. Finally found the B&B, but then it is already so late that we urgently need to go to Mik's.

At the bus stop (yes, it's raining again) Ciska discovers Ian, who is gobsmacked to see us. We make an appointment with him for tomorrow.

On to Mik's house. Present also are his girlfriend and a good friend of his, and he plays us the new album, which sounds excellent. We stay for tea, Mik cooks, and in the evening we all go to a pub, which Kevin and his girlfriend come to as well. When the pub closes, Mik and girlfriend and us go to Kev's house, where we drink an alcoholic banana-mash drink, which Kev picked up in the Bahama's, and watch Music Box for hours. Taxi back to the B&B.

Tuesday August 19

According to Mik, Andy will be home from Crete tonight, so we decide to stay for one more day. So: back to the bus station to have our coach ticket changed to Wednesday. Then on to Ian, who lives in a dump and gives us awful 'coffee', and plays us things on guitar and synthesizer. Then he gives us a tour of Sheffield, eats chips with baked beans (yuck!), and we take pictures of the city.

He shows us the Comsats' rehearsal room, and he and Ciska play the piano together. He walks us back to the station to get our rucksacks, because we didn't have time to collect them the day before. And he takes us to the bus stop, while telling us about his ex-girlfriend who left him after last year's Comsat tour. He really is a sweetie.

In the evening we've agreed to go to the pub again and we first pick up Mik and his girlfriend. Steve is also coming to the pub, how is this all possible!

No, of course, it isn't possible. Steve is sitting at a small table with his girlfriend and waves back, but that's it.

Huge discussion again about extra guitarists, ugh. Afterwards with Mik and his girlfriend back to their house for coffee. Later Steve plus girlfriend show up too, to ring a taxi from there.

We end up with the four of us, which is a lot of fun until Mik drinks too much, and becomes rather insufferable. He slams everything and everyone and I don't like it (him).

Still, there's the interesting announcement that Frank is coming to Sheffield the next day for a band meeting and that afterwards he could give us a lift to London in his car.

Andy not back yet.

Wednesday August 20

Back to the bus station again, after we've said goodbye to the people in the bed and breakfast, and returned the coach tickets. We still get 12 pounds back from the 15 pounds we paid, not bad.

We try to ring Andy to ask if he could come a little earlier to Mr. Kites, the bar where the meeting is, and where we have agreed to meet the band at three o'clock, so that we can talk to him alone for a bit. Andy doesn't answer the phone.

Around noon we show up at Mr. Kites. We drink coffee, leave our rucksacks there, and go to a second-hand bookshop nearby. Then we eat a tuna sandwich in the famous sandwich bar under the rehearsal room.

At three pm Mik appears, who apologises (which is good) for the previous evening, because he realised that I was a bit upset by everything he said. And then Andy arrives.

Oh no! We don't want to go to London in Knarf's car, we want to stay here! Five minutes of Andy is definitely not enough. Andy suggests we phone him later to set up an appointment. We do. And we let Knarf drive back to London by himself.

In the evening we show up at Andy's house to go out with him and his wife – what a woman of the world. We bought 'Narziss and Gold-mund' by Hermann Hesse for him in the bookshop. Such a beautiful book. Tomorrow it's his birthday again.

After the pub he plays us some home movies of early Comsat tours. (Making a Knarf snowman and then pelting it with snowballs, ha ha.) And we look at all his scrapbooks and photo albums of the band. And read the application letter Kevin wrote hoping to join the Comsats.

Poor Andy – back from his holidays at 1 pm, a meeting with Knarf at 3 pm and then on until 2 the next morning. How tired he must be! We are also tired, but happy that we are still in Sheffield. So tired that at night Ciska sighs: 'Just imagine, four hours with a car in Knarf!'

Thursday August 21
And again we go to the bus station, but this time to buy a new coach ticket. Dumped rucksacks and spent the rest of the morning shopping and buying some postcards of Sheffield.

We take the bus at a quarter to three, get to London at seven, kill a few hours in a pub and go back to Holland on the Budget Bus at ten.

Oh, how we sleep! Three nights in a row in bed at 3 or 4 am and still up at 7.30 am to eat baked beans, unappetizing sausages and fried eggs. It's called Bed *and* Breakfast after all.

Friday August 22
Around half past 11 we're at The Hague Central Station, have a coffee there and go home on the tram. Unpack, shower, take film roll no. 4 with Sheffield on it to the 1-hour photo service and collect it, and then… sleep!!

A mouse with a tail
Two months later we are once again attending a gig at the Horse, and to our surprise we bump into Caspar. We don't have his address, so we've never been able to ask him how things turned out in London. He shouts in Ciska's ear that they have indeed been to see How we Live and that he has received a note for us from Steve-2. He also took

pictures at the gig. Our attention to the Chameleons gig in progress slackens considerably.

Afterwards, when silence has returned, Caspar tells us that they walked into the dressing room after the London gig, but did not find anyone there. They discovered Steve-2 at the bar. They addressed him and Steve recognised them immediately, because during gigs he always pays close attention to the audience, so he had already spotted them taking photos. They had told him that they had been sent to the Marquee by two girls they had met at a gig in The Hague, and that they sent their love. 'Oh, Ciska and Inge', said Steve, without any help from them.

This came as a bit of a surprise to Lex and Caspar, who'd actually assumed that we had been bragging. When they told Steve about our near-fight, whether to stay in London or take the bus, he decided to write us a note.

They hadn't liked the gig very much. Caspar thought we should be glad we didn't go. He is, of course, completely wrong about this.

The following week we visit him at home to collect the note:
'Now then, Ciska, what's all this about going to Sheffield when we're playing in London? Inge was right!
Love & kisses to you.
Enjoy yourself in the U.K.
Steve xx'

Aw, that Steve-2.

A stack of emotions

Today the new album finally came out. It's called *Chasing Shadows* and has a nice, stylish cover with a vague black and white photo. How beautiful it is. I'm perfectly happy, although I couldn't hold back the tears when I heard *The Cutting Edge* for the first time. That song brings back so many memories. When we went to see Mik that first day, there was pouring rain, and he played us the new album for the first time. Today it also rained heavily and the second song on the album is *The Cutting Edge*. I closed my eyes and was back in Mik's living room. And in the background the rain... I was almost certain that if I opened my eyes I'd be back in Sheffield.

'Lord help me I'm mystified, it seems I got the cutting edge'

When *Pray for Rain* played, I was back at Andy's house the day we watched his home movies and then listened to that song at twilight. So many emotions.

I tried to ring Ciska many times, but she was not at home. Eventually she called back and she understands exactly what I mean. It is such a strange idea that no one on earth, not even the Comsats themselves, can understand what this album means to us. Everyone can find it very beautiful, but that special feeling, so tied up with memories, belongs only to Ciska and me.

I am now on my sixth spin, and although I should really be writing essays, I just can't help but listen to the Comsats.

The latest OOR mentioned that in December they would come to Vaals, Sneek and Amsterdam. I was very much looking forward to that. I also planned to go all three times, I had already looked up the trains from Vaals (in the deep south) to Sneek (in the very north). I was so looking forward to it. And now it turns out that the tour has been cancelled.

They are rescheduled to come at the end of January or early February next year. I really hope so. Winter in Vaals again. Of course.

Thrills and spills

Multicoloured hair

I discovered a while ago that if I put 'Superblonde' on my dyed black hair, the black turns orange, and the roots become very light blond. Last week I tried to dye multicoloured hair, but failed. I was blond at the back with an occasional orange streak, but it hadn't taken everywhere. You hardly even saw it from the front.

I bleached my hair again this morning with Superblonde and then dyed it. This time it worked well. Very much so. I am now completely peroxide blond (white) with bright orange ends on top. It was a big shock when I first looked in the mirror, but now I'm almost beginning to like it.

Oh, and the Comsats are coming! First Vaals, then Koog aan de Zaan or Noord-Scharwoude (the magazines don't agree on that) and finally the Paradiso.

The evening before (January 1987)

The tour starts tomorrow. I'm not nervous, but strangely enough I can't really imagine seeing them tomorrow. I am looking forward to it, but it feels so different from normal. We cremated granny yesterday and that hurts a lot. I feel rough and sad, and on the one hand I don't want to go to Vaals at all, and on the other hand I hope this tour cheers me up a bit. After all, my own life does not stop, even if my favourite grandmother is gone.

Vaals

As usual, on the train to Vaals the four of us attract a lot of attention. The whole compartment stares at us, some disapproving, others find it amusing. Ciska has also just been through some personal drama, but we have resolved not to act depressed. That is not very difficult, because seeing the Comsats means getting away from all our misery for a while.

From Sittard we take the train to Heerlen, then the bus to Vaals and on to Piet Haan. We do some last-minute 'repainting' and hairspray spraying, and at 9 o'clock take the bus back to Vaals and walk – cold, cold, cold – on slippery streets to the Spuugh.

It's a thrill to be in the venue and know that the Comsats will come on soon. The gig starts and, well, we should have known better: the Comsats make emotional music, so you can try and keep a straight face, but alas. They mainly play the new album, nothing light from the Jive era, and four songs from the old doom era. We had hoped to be cheered up by the gig, but almost all songs are emotionally charged and heavy. When *Pray for Rain* starts, it all becomes too much and we flee to the back of the room.

Steve is also having a hard time. After a few songs something goes wrong with his voice. The high notes won't come out in any case, and every time he opens his mouth everything starts to squeak and grind so badly that sometimes no sound comes out at all.

After an hour they decide to pack it in because he just has no voice left.

During the gig I have decided that I don't want to go to the dressing room, because I feel so sad and I really can't sit there and act happy. I'm afraid if someone asks me how I'm doing, I'll burst into tears. But my friends persuade me to come along.

Inside, Mik and Andy are being interviewed, and Nahna and Caroline go to talk to Kevin. I look at Steve with a 'you poor boy' look and go over to him. Ciska does too. There's only one chair next to him and Ciska sits down, and well, Steve only talks to one person at a time.

Ciska explains to him about the set, that we really didn't need to hear it right now. Well, Steve is not at all happy about that, because they have just decided that they definitely don't want to be a pop band anymore, and now there are complaints already?

Ciska tells him that we have been through quite a lot in the last few weeks and were in desperate need of cheerful songs. Steve is on the verge of either getting seriously interested or talking over it all. He decides on the middle ground and says in a somewhat non-tactful but well-meaning way: 'Problems? How old are you anyway?' According to him, everything gets better as you get older. Oh yeah? 'I'm already 23 and I have problems too, so when does that 'things start to get better' begin?' I ask. 'Just after that,' says Steve. Fine, now we know. Why shouldn't 'little girls' have problems? 'You're still smiling,' Steve says. In other words, it can't be that bad.

The next day they were supposed to play in Noord-Scharwoude, but now they are suddenly going to Hamburg to record a live tv show. And that with a singer who has no voice.

No voice, still sexy

I am tired and happy, and have collapsed, all at once. So much has happened, and I feel so confused! My lasting memory of this tour will surely be about Steve. What a huge improvement there.

Paradiso Amsterdam is my thirtieth Comsat gig, and of course the milestone has to be celebrated. So after the gig we go on one of our pub crawls with Mik and Andy until the early hours. I am not that much of a party animal really, but I do enjoy these nights out in such pleasant company.

Two years ago I told Andy in a café that I would so like to talk to Steve. Now, with some drinks behind me I am sitting next to my confessor again, and this time I feel the need to tell him that I think Steve is so sexy. The concept is clearly new to Andy, and he finds it totally incomprehensible but very very funny. And of course the next day the gossip tells Steve.

Fortunately Steve responds well. At first I find the idea unnerving, but hey, if Andy gossiping means that Steve talks to me and kisses me goodbye, then I really don't regret my revelation.

Andy also provides the best Comsat quote of all time. He talks about gigs in Germany and how the German audience reacts, compared to Dutch and English audiences:

In Germany, we always count the Zoogabays.
Let that sink in for a while. I still think it's genius.

Steve in Rotterdam, februari 1987

Because Steve has a very bad cold and his voice isn't really coming back, the tour is cut short. Very sad for everything and everyone, but especially for Steve. He feels guilty because his 'instrument' isn't working and people are not getting their money's worth, he thinks. And no matter how many times people tell him: 'Just because your voice is bad doesn't automatically mean that the whole gig is bad', he still suffers. In Amsterdam he goes to see a doctor.

Noord-Scharwoude was to come after Vaals, but that's become a tv show in Hamburg, Paradiso goes ahead, Tilburg is cancelled, Rotterdam almost as well, but fortunately in the end it isn't. And from that final night of the tour I have a few dressing-room photos, one of which is of myself with Steve. The embarrassed look on my face is absolutely brilliant. It still makes me giggle. As does my ridiculous hair colour.

Six months later
A postcard from Andy lands on the doormat, sent from Houston, Texas, where they are playing that day. Everyone is having a good time, he writes, and they've played everywhere in America he's ever heard of. We are coming to the festival next month, aren't we?

P.S. Got it yet, the Zoogabays? If Germans want an encore after a gig, they don't shout, as we do in Holland, 'We want more!'. No, in Germany you hear everyone shout: Zugabe! Zugabe!

In love with Holland

More than forty years after we first met, I am sitting at Andy's kitchen table and tell him I'm writing a book about my Comsat adventures. I have a question which I never thought about before, I say, but which actually fascinates me now.

Did you have fans like us in Germany as well? People who basically travelled the country with you, went to almost every gig, always showed up at sound checks and came through the dressing-room door afterwards. Fans you went out for a drink with after a gig? Were there German equivalents of us anywhere, or were we unique? After all, you toured there almost as often as in Holland.

No, says Andy, there weren't any. We did have loyal fans, who bought a ticket to see us on every tour, and sometimes someone would walk into our dressing room wanting an autograph or who had a question, but like you? No, not at all. We only had that in Holland.

During our first Dutch tour in September 1979, which lasted two weeks, we just fell in love with Holland. And that feeling remained. And then we became friends with you, which made the touring even more enjoyable. As you've noticed, we couldn't stay away from Holland. For us you belonged to the 'touring in Holland' feeling. A sense of coming home.

Andy 1987

Staying with Mik, staying with Andy

In the summer of 1987 Ciska and I go to Edinburgh again and then on to Sheffield. Mik has very sweetly invited us to come and stay at his house this time. Wow, but this is fun! We should definitely do this more often.

We like the Edinburgh-plus-Sheffield concept, so a year later we repeat the trip a third time. My trusty diary knows the details.

August 1988

We took the night bus and arrived at a quarter to five in the morning at the well-known bus station. We were the only ones who got off the bus, the station was deserted, lots of rain, and no phone box in sight. I hadn't thought of that possibility. Were approached by a policeman who thought we looked very suspicious at this late hour, found a phone after all, called and fortunately were quickly picked up by Mik in his car. It's just great that he stays up late into the night for us. Now that's what I call hospitality.

After a short night, at breakfast, Mik put on the tape of the new LP as promised. Well, first of all it was on volume far-too-loud, let me blame a large part of my initial dismay on that, but still, the music itself was also incredibly loud. At times it seemed almost heavy metal.

Mik's girlfriend had already secretly told us that it was aimed at the American market, something that no Comsat himself would admit of course, but which was also quite obvious without any explanations. I occasionally drew a parallel with Springsteen. Just the titles themselves: *The Gun is Loaded* and *Born Again*, how American can you get? One song even had a real guitar solo!

Mik is never very good with criticism, but Andy does want to hear things, so I explained to him later that I thought it was such a shame that the subtlety of the earlier albums was gone. This was really like having a wall of sound coming at you. Too many instruments at once, too loud, and the final effect (at least to me) was pure noise.

The next morning I got up early to play the tape twice by myself, at a more normal volume, and then I liked most of the songs a bit better.

I understand that Andy had wanted us to stay at his place this time, but we didn't know that, so we never contacted him. Well, that's it then, after two such great times staying at Mik's house, next time we're going to find out how things are at Andy residence.

Another news item, and very essential, is that the Comsats have finally dumped Knarf. But they are by no means rid of him. I don't quite understand how it all works, but Frank has hired an expensive solicitor to strip the Comsats. He wants £20,000 for breach of contract, whereas he himself was the first to hint that they should break the tie. It now appears that he also, without them knowing, once signed a contract about publishing rights. A real detective has now been hired to track down that contract. Island Records is willing to help with a loan to pay Frank off, but that other matter must be taken care of first.

Or something like that, I don't really understand everything, but considering that Andy said he was happy that the mortgage on their house was in his wife's name, things must be dire.

The album was ready by the end of April, but will probably not be released until early next year, if all goes well. So, many worries. And touring, forget it.

Over coffee I asked Mik if they had any plans for the day, and Mik said Andy had invited us for tea, but that was only around half four and nothing was planned before that. So we mumbled something about liking the countryside, and yes, wow, we went onto the moors. It turns out that Mik and his girlfriend like walking as much as we do, so that is quite a bonus. Something else we have in common.

Dropped off at Andy's. Mik had been teasing me a few times that Andy was probably going to cook mussels. That's what he poisoned me with last year, and I've heard from several people that he felt quite bad about that afterwards. Poor Mik, I never blamed him.

Andy had made lasagne, which was absolutely delicious, and chocolate mousse for dessert.

During coffee the word 'essay' was mentioned and Andy went all overboard. He explained to his wife: 'When we are on tour in Holland and we enter a venue, Inge is always sitting there with a book in her lap. You ask her if she wants to go for a drink, but no, she's been there since noon and she's already written three essays, and she has two more to finish before the gig starts. I've never seen her at a sound check without a book. She has written about 150 essays in as long as I've known her.'

What an endless imagination he has. But it's sweet that he makes all this up. Nevertheless, that's enough now, Andy.

Finally we watched a video of a tv report about their new own studio, which they can rent out to other bands when they're not using it themselves. So, a good investment. If only Frank won't…

In the evening, as usual, to the pub, even Kev had been summoned, but he was acting insufferably arrogant and annoying. I didn't pay him too much attention. Andy was wonderfully cheerful and silly. When I went to the toilet, he said, 'Ah, you're going to revisit last year's happy memories.' And yes, last year I had ample time to study the toilet extensively. I was in there about twenty times, I think. Those bloody mussels. How awful I felt then, on the very night that Steve came out to the pub especially for me, because I'd asked again and again, something which he normally never does.

After closing time everyone went back to Mik's house for coffee. Andy and Mik had had four pints each and acted accordingly. They started to reminisce about gigs in Holland. Every now and then we were all howling with laughter.

Another nice thing: we've won after all. It's 1-0 to us: Andy said very subtly that they might take on an extra guitarist for the upcoming live work. I almost didn't believe my ears, the four sworn Comsats who are the only four who can make music and the rest of the world doesn't understand – these same four Comsats are seriously thinking about an extra guitarist again?

Andy had also thought of a new method for testing him. Two

weeks of driving around with the five of them in a van, no playing, just driving, and if he could behave, didn't complain, etc., then he could stay. Whether he could play guitar well was only an after-thought.

Hospitality to the very end: Mik drove us all the way to Hull, from where the ferry was sailing. He got nostalgic tour feelings when he saw the boat, and I hope he will soon be able to board that ferry again himself.

November, same year
Staying with Andy for three nights! It all began in late September when I sent a copy of my graduation thesis to Andy and mentioned in the accompanying letter that he might see us before the end of the year. This was followed up on a memorable Sunday in late October when Ciska bravely picked up the phone, and after some trouble with wrong numbers, got through to Andy and announced that we were indeed planning to come to Sheffield ('Great!' said Andy) and that three weekends suited us best. He looked at his diary and con-cluded that the first weekend, mid-November, was fine. We promised to send a postcard with further details, that we would arrive on the Friday, and see you soon.

So, on the boat, as usual the North Sea Ferries to Hull, the boat where you will eat yourself completely sick, both in the evening and in the morning, because all the food is included in the price. Which is why we sat in the bar later feeling quite queasy, especially when there was some rough weather. But apart from that everything was great. We were so full of anticipation and so excited.

I had written to Andy that we would come around four o'clock, so we had almost the whole day to fill. First to the post office to get some money, where we walked to without having to check the map. Some-thing we were acting tough about, but were secretly very proud of.
   Then past all the beloved spots towards Mr. Kites. We felt com-pletely at home there again. Steve's girlfriend works there, so we

Still in black. Graduation picture 1988

approached her and told her that we were the Dutch girls that always follow the Comsats. She was very surprised and asked if we were staying with Mik again. No, we said, with Andy. She said she'd tell Steve we were there.

When we arrived at his house Andy said they had tickets to a Mahler concert that night, but that we could come along if we wanted. There were still a few tickets left, so off we went to Sheffield City Hall. We sat on the second balcony, at the very top, far away from Andy and his wife, but the concert was truly magnificent.

Afterwards we went to the pub. There we found Mik and his girl-friend, Mik's friend we had met before, and also Nick, the intended new guitarist. I had a long chat with him, and discovered that he is in fact just like us, a loyal fan from the early days. He told me about his Comsat posters, badges, singles and an unknown number of illegally obtained (i.e. nicked from the rehearsal room) tapes. And he will go on tour with them to America (probably in January), and he had never been abroad. I think if I became the new guitar player I would react just the way he did. Nice little thing was that Andy introduced us as 'old friends from Holland'.

The next day was a typical Sheffield Saturday in the city centre, according to Andy, who would like to have an electronic stick to poke slow-walking grannies with. And indeed, it was terribly busy on the street and in the shops. As every day, in the evening we ended up in the pub again.

When we left the pub it was raining heavily, or no, it was sleet. Just imagine that tomorrow there might be a thick layer of snow, I said. No, everyone said, it's just wet snow.

Next morning at Andy's suggestion we weren't to get up before eleven. But at 9 am I was awakened by the scraping sound of a shovel on the street. After twenty minutes I went to have a look, and everything was stark white. So it had really snowed. I got up, went downstairs and put on the tape of the new album for the umpteenth time. We can take it home with us, Andy said. Really!

In the evening I helped Andy in the kitchen chopping up the vegetables for the casserole that followed. Yum, yum. In the kitchen my eye suddenly fell on the calendar that was hanging there and the numbers 18, 19, 20 were circled and it said 'DG' in fat green letters. Look at that, the Dutch girls are coming. Little things like that are always nice to discover. Cooking food together also gave me a wonderful feeling of connection.

Snow in Sheffield

By the way, both Mik and Andy are clearly so homesick for Holland, where, if it's up to the record company, they really won't be going for a while. So Andy and his lovely missus have planned to go on holiday to the Netherlands next August. I'm all for it! We can cook for them for a change.

Andy suggested we walk down to the video shop and rent a movie for after the pub. So the three of us hit the slippery streets again in the dark. We walked down a street, and Andy was the first to almost fall, but he just held his own. Ciska just after that really fell on the ground, and we hadn't even turned the corner before I slid past. All very funny.

In the evening it was back to the pub. I'm not sure of the conversations that went back and forth, because I was so sleepy I was barely present. All I can remember is Mik's terribly silly joke, about a drunken man on the ferry to Belgium, who addressed someone on the boat and asked where he was going. 'Ostend' was the answer, to which the man said: 'What a coincidence, so am I', after which Mik himself almost fell under the table with laughter, which was ten times funnier than the joke itself. What a delightful man he is.

Mik 1987

Mik took us home to Andy's in his car. In the afternoon in the video shop, I was given the honour of selecting a movie. It became one with my hero Mickey Roarke in it. Now in the car, Andy wondered aloud why on earth women found Mickey Roarke so sexy. I understand why men don't understand that, but exactly because he looks clever and yet like a *clochard*, he's cute. I said it might make things more clear if I said I liked M.R. for more or less the same reasons that I liked Steve. To which the gentlemen said that Steve's cuteness was really rather overrated. 'You've never lived in the same house as Steve, so you don't know what you're talking about.' 'No, I haven't, but I'm willing to try', I said.

That shut them up.

Arrived at Andy's, we watched the movie Angel Heart. I think Andy had even more fun watching us than we did with the movie itself. That film was so bloody scary that we were constantly on the edge of the sofa and occasionally we got such a start that we really screamed or jumped up with fright.

Monday. At breakfast we already start to feel a little sentimental. Only a few hours to go and then we're going on the ferry back to Holland. Andy has promised us that, before taking us to the station, he will show us their new studio.

The mood is already getting a bit tense. Andy talks about touring and the record company, and that everything is getting a bit tricky, especially now with the name change. I suddenly wake up, 'the name change?' Then it is Andy's turn to be surprised. They haven't been called The Comsat Angels for over six months now. No?? What are they called then?

'Headhunters,' we repeat in horror, after staring at him for ten seconds. Headhunters? How is it possible that no one told us? Well, it is a fact that in August I had already seen the term Headhunters written on the cover of the tape, but I had automatically assumed it was the title of the album. Not one single hair on my head would have thought that it could be they themselves. Still, it's lucky that we discovered this (half an hour) before we left. Otherwise we could

- 136 -

have asked for the new Comsat album forever, and we might not even have shown up when they played in Holland, because we wouldn't know it was them.

To the studio. We weren't even through the door when Andy said: 'Hey, that's Kev's briefcase, so he's back'. We didn't like this announcement. In our current mood, Kevin was the last person we wanted to see. But luckily he was out for coffee.

The studio was indeed very beautiful and looked quite sophisticated. Andy explained how the studio had been built, what was so special about it, and so on.

We arrived at the station half an hour early and I would have preferred Andy to go home, because I was about to burst into tears. But no, he still wanted to have coffee with us, and then he bought a platform ticket and came on the train with us. Oh, how unhappy I felt, I couldn't say anything anymore, I just wanted to stay in Sheffield forever.

Andy felt it, announced he was going, said he had enjoyed it all so much, kissed us both, walked to the door, looked back, passed outside our window, looked back again, and was gone. And then my tears began to flow. The whole train looked at me, but I didn't care, I just couldn't hold it in any longer.

When I got home I really cried for a week, I felt so terribly 'homesick'. I played the tape of the new album all day long, and I did a very creative drawing of Andy the day after returning home. I think it's pretty good. A small miniature, and it is now in a frame.

Well, that's it. I wrote 24 pages about the trip, and still it's not enough. I'm afraid I'll have to write a book about 'My life with the Comsats' one day. It's a shame though that only seven copies will be sold (to the Comsats and my friends).

P.S. In the end the new name did not become Headhunters after all. A year later, the tape we took home was released as a CD by Dream Command. The tracks with the American titles were no longer on it.

Interview for OOR

Years go by and the Comsats are still busy making music, but unfortunately no one is aware of this. I've almost given up hope too, and don't think I'll ever see them on stage again. A new record also seems out of the question, because after the Dream Command CD was released they lost their record deal.

In recent years they worked on new songs and recordings in their own Axis Studios in Sheffield. Without a record company that keeps shouting 'time is money' and 'hurry up!', it was nice to just work away. They could take their time and decide for themselves. If necessary, they could do something twenty times over, it didn't matter. An album is now ready, almost finished, and it sounds just fantastic, so I'm told.

Miracles do happen
A recently founded Dutch record company, Crisis, contacts them and asks how the band is doing, if they even still exist. It is now 1992.

The deal is closed quickly. It's great news. I am secretly also a little chuffed that it is a Dutch record company that dares to take them on. Right, I think, the Dutch are still leading the way.

My next thought is: could I myself do something to help, some promotional thing to bring attention to the forthcoming album? For a while now I've been writing as a freelancer for some local newspapers, and I come up with a cunning plan.

Music paper OOR used to write very positively about the Comsats, so I hope that interest is still there somewhere. I contact them and ask if I can do an interview with the reborn Comsats. 'Fine with us,' OOR says, 'go ahead. But we can't guarantee we'll print it.'

I ring Andy to say I want to come over and interview them, and a month later I go to Sheffield on my own for the first time. Ciska can't come along due to other obligations, so I'm going to stay with Andy for a week all by myself. The interview is scheduled for the last day.

It is a great shock to hear that Mik has left the band, for reasons that are unclear to me. I visit him at home, sit with him in his backyard and listen to his story.

The interview takes place in their studio. Steve, Kevin and Andy are present, Mik is not. It's going to be the first time in five years I'm going to see Steve. Andy laughs at me because I'm a bit nervous about that.

In the studio there are glass walls and glass doors everywhere, so you can see people four rooms away. Steve is sitting a few rooms away, sees me enter, gets up and comes straight over. He says 'Hello Inge, how are you?' and kisses me. I am flabbergasted; there is no other word for it.

What a change, both in his appearance and in behaviour. He's aged and looks a little faded, but that's nothing compared to the inner change. He talks and talks, and laughs, and even puts an arm around my shoulders. Carry me out of the room on a stretcher.

But no, don't, I'm here to do an interview. So I grab my list of questions from my bag, turn on my tape recorder and get going.

Andy, Steve and Kevin in their studio, 1992

The interview: a band with nine lives

'Yeah, it has been a long time, hasn't it? Just when you thought it was safe to go into a record shop...' Keyboard player Andy Peake makes a joke of it, but the undertone is serious. The Comsat Angels have been gone for a long time. It has been five years since they were last seen on a Dutch stage. What has happened since then? Singer Steve Fellows explains.

'We had a lot of business problems. We were with Island Records, but the relationship between us and Island got worse and worse. They did nothing for us anymore. Politics, you know.'

One of the problems The Comsat Angels had was with their name. The American company Communication Satellite Inc. had forbidden the name 'Comsat' in America. And so the band changed their name.

'At the time it seemed like a good idea,' says Steve. 'Unfortunately, it mainly had a bad effect, because nobody knew the new name'.

So what was the name?

'Dream Command... yeah yeah, I know. We made a CD under that name, *Fire on the Moon*, but it didn't go down too well either. It was just a very strange, confusing period of time.'

And now you're called The Comsat Angels again?

'Yes, except in America, where we are called The C.S. Angels.'

Aren't we one band member short?

'Unfortunately Mik left us a few months ago. He was very disappointed, because everything came to a standstill. He was terribly frustrated by that. But he still played on the new songs, and we are still good friends, you know.'

Soon your new CD will be released, entitled *My Mind's Eye*. Is that 'old-fashioned' Comsat music or have you changed a lot?

'In a way it's very similar to the early Comsat material, but the songs are better. The first three albums were made in a wave of enthusiasm. Then we started experimenting in different directions. We wanted to try and expand our possibilities, but it didn't work very well. In the end, we realised that what we most like to play is also what is most appreciated by other people. The new songs are in fact direct descendants of the first albums.'

Andy Peake adds: 'We were steered in the wrong direction by all sorts of factors, but now we just follow our own instincts.'

It all sounds hopeful, but why is it suddenly possible again?

Steve Fellows: 'Since the split with Island, we started jamming a lot again, just like before, and most of the songs come from that. We had no special purpose and no contract, so we were totally relaxed. We just played and it felt good, no one was spurring us on.'

Resulting in a new contract, with the Dutch Crisis label. How did that happen?

Bass player Kevin Bacon: 'It's a new label, set up by people who worked at Polydor when we were under contract there. They originally contacted us because they wanted to reissue some of our old LPs on CD. But then we told them about our new material, and of course they wanted that even more.'

Perhaps an awkward question: The Comsat Angels were once very well known on the Dutch club circuit. Do you think you can still build on that old reputation?

Steve Fellows looks a bit annoyed when he answers. 'No, of course you can't count on anything. But I hope people will listen to the new CD, because it's really good stuff. We certainly don't expect everyone to remember us, but they don't have to. The CD speaks for itself.'

I'm getting really curious now. Please tell me about the style of the new songs.

Steve laughs. 'Difficult to describe. We did this CD purely for the love of it. With the Dream Command album we thought: if we just make it a bit glossier and make it more commercial, we might earn more. But it wasn't real, you know, it wasn't the Comsats. Now we are back on track.'

Yes, Steve, but how does it *sound?*

'Hm, the songs are quite varied. Some songs are all guitar, and others have just fleeting sounds. I think it's important how a CD is built up, from atmosphere to atmosphere, and from feeling to feeling. I can't say what kind of music it is as a whole, it's about the mood.'

Is this your final attempt or are you unbreakable?

'You never know, do you? But even if no one at all bought *My Mind's Eye*, we'll keep going. We never stop, no. You get your strength from the music and the CD is good, so we definitely feel confident.'

So you see a bright future?

'Yes absolutely. There are several things on the agenda again. The new CD, a single, *Driving*, and in the autumn there will also be a CD with radio sessions we have done for the BBC over the years.'

Does anyone want to say one last thing?

'Listen to the CD. Anyone who has even the slightest curiosity about the band, listen, because it's our best work. You'll like it, trust me!'

Too bad
The editor-in-chief of OOR decides not to publish my piece, the nincompoop. Time for revenge!

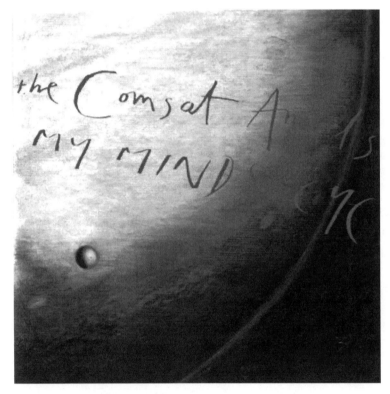

'And all the stars they shine so bright'

A new beginning

My Mind's Eye is released in the autumn of 1992 and a Dutch tour is announced for early the following year, for the first time in six years. Yes! Yes!, I think, the good times will come again, life will be beautiful once more. I am so looking forward to it. With a bit of tension though, because the line-up of the band has changed once again. Mik has had a change of heart and has come back. Hurrah, very good news! But now Kevin has decided to hang up his bass. He is more interested in production work and finds doing both too complicated.

So Kevin has left the band (Kev, the only one I could spare if necessary) and has been replaced by a new bass player, Terry Todd. A second guitarist has also been added, one Simon Anderson. I've never heard of either one, so I'm very curious. A five-piece band, who could ever have imagined it?

The first gig is in late January 1993. With some trepidation, in the afternoon Ciska and I go to the venue. I have to get used to things again, and I also don't like Terry and Simon straight away. But nothing can temper my joy of knowing that tonight I will get to see Mik *and* Andy *and* Steve on stage again.

Ciska and I go to a café for a bit and come back an hour later when they are sound checking. We take a seat on a bench at the back of the venue. Steve, who wasn't there an hour ago, suddenly notices us. He waves, gestures 'five minutes', and looks pleased to see us. My interview meeting last year has prepared me a little, but Ciska is looking at Steve with eyes like saucers. And would you believe it, a little later he comes over, kisses us both and says, 'So tell me, how are you?' Truly a metamorphosis.

The gig also takes a little getting used to. They mainly focus on the new stuff, which fits in well with the popular style of the time, rather grungy. The excitement the music brings is fantastic. Louder, harder, sweatier – it's like a work-out at the gym, but far more enjoyable. People can't stand still for long, they dance, they jump. Fun is had by all.

They are here for three days and then go to Germany for a week, come back to Holland for a few days for gigs all over the country, and then return to Germany. This routine will take a month in total. Back and forth, back and forth; as far as I'm concerned we could keep doing this forever.

The first time we say goodbye because they're going east, I happen to walk with them to their van, because I'm carrying something that belongs to a band member. There we say goodbye for a week. 'Have fun in Germany, and knock 'em dead.' Not just me, but also Mik and Andy don't believe their eyes when Steve squeezes me as if I'm a lemon.

Many well-known places are revisited on this tour. It's party time again at a sold-out Paradiso. It is clear that the audience welcomes the new music with open arms. We privately celebrate the successful comeback until the early hours. Four band members and four girls are having an exuberant pub crawl through Amsterdam. (No revelations this time.)

A few days later they do a live radio recording in the afternoon, where an audience is present. It's really going in the right direction again. Haarlem is sold out, Utrecht feels like 'old times', and then there are the gigs at the Horse and in Leiden, where all the loyal old fans are present, but there's also an influx of new ones. We write on the wall of the Leiden dressing room: *Comsats back to stay!*

Everyone is happy, everything's going so well.

Steve's new behaviour is permanent, I notice. He keeps coming over to chat, and when he sees someone about to take a picture of him and me, he kisses my cheek at just the right moment. I still can't quite believe it all, but I look at the photo again and conclude: the proof is there.

Steve, Ciska and I backstage at the LVC, Leiden, 1993

After a short adjustment period the two new band members, Terry and Simon, turn out to be an asset, especially Terry. He is sweet and caring. On a day off from their busy tour schedule, all Comsats, except for Steve who has gone to Germany for an interview, take the train to Delft. Ciska receives them at her place, and a while later we move to mine. This is something we have hoped for for so many years. After all those times staying at their homes in Sheffield, now finally the Comsats come to ours. It feels like a crown on twelve years of friendship.

The last day of this first come-back tour is in Brussels, and this happens to be my 40th Comsat gig. To celebrate the milestone, I had a pastry shop decorate a cake with the text '40 Comsat gigs'. After the gig, when everyone else has left, I offer the cake to the band. They are very surprised. Forty, really? You have seen us forty times already? Mik says. Steve, who has already gone to sleep, is dragged out of bed by Mik, because of course he has to be there to celebrate, too. In utter amazement he eats a piece of cake. The ceremonial aspect of the event works well.

The band are staying in the same building where the venue is located, and there is exactly one small room with a bunk bed left, so Ciska and I can also spend the night there. The evening ends with a nightly farewell party. Without Steve, because he's already back on one ear.

In the morning we all have breakfast together and the tour is officially over. The band give us a lift in their van back to Holland. I manage to get a seat next to Steve and we occasionally chat a bit.

In the end Ciska and I decide to stay in the van all the way to Rotterdam, where they take the ferry home, so that we can wave them off after this great tour.

It's a pretty tearful goodbye. Everyone gets out of the van and many hugs are exchanged. Steve is standing a little to the side and looks at the ground. When everyone has hugged everyone else and I've just decided 'right, what was I thinking', he approaches Ciska, and kisses her goodbye.

I'm last. He looks at me with a deeply sad look. Of course I don't look very happy either, because the long-awaited tour is over and I'm very bad at saying goodbye. Before I always trusted that they would be back in no time, so I was never very sad, but now I'm not so sure anymore. What if this was it, and nothing more will follow? Steve throws himself around my neck, doesn't want to let go, lets go anyway, looks at me even more sadly, embraces me again, and doesn't let go for a long time. When he does, there are tears in his eyes.

Two seconds after the van has driven onto the ferry I break down. What a tour, what a band, what good music, what lovely people. I love the Comsats like no other band on earth.

The end

It ended like this.

The Comsats tour the Netherlands very intensively for another number of years, a brilliant last CD comes out, called *The Glamour*, but eventually the plug is pulled. The party is over.

Goodbye band, goodbye gigs, goodbye fan club.

Nothing lasts forever, I know, but still it is very sad. It was such an excellent band. I have seen the Comsats play precisely 65 times.

Ciska and I continue to spend a week in Sheffield every summer; that fortunately remains unchanged. But our mutual touring life with the Comsats is over.

But then… unexpectedly, this century, I end up with 70 gigs after all.

Sleep No More for a week or two

All good things come to those who wait

It's Sunday 26 April, Sheffield, O2 Academy. This is the big day. Today The Comsat Angels play their first gig in 14 years. No one in the whole wide world believed it was possible. But, the miracle has happened, and over 600 people (from all over that same wide world) are here to cheer the band on, to meet old and new friends and to have the best night of 2009.

It's a very special gig. Not just because the band play only songs from their first three albums – the ones that most fans agree contain their very best work – they play them in the original line-up, too. It's the four men who recorded these original three albums that we see on stage here tonight, giving their all, making the moody magic of *Waiting for a Miracle*, *Sleep No More* and *Fiction* come to life.

At any Comsat gig in the past there was a fan base present. And then there were people who just dropped by, not quite knowing what to expect, any excuse to drink beer. Well, this lot seem to be absent now. This time only the real fans, the appreciative ones are here. This creates an enormous sense of elation, with the audience almost shivering with anticipation.

The atmosphere inside the O2 Academy is fantastic. The whole place seems to be sizzling. Everyone's waiting, hoping, expecting to be amazed, and silently anxious that it may therefore be a bit of a disappointment.

It's my first Comsats live experience in 14 years. I am one of these people who were sadly convinced they would never see this great band in action ever again. I haven't been able to sleep for all of last week. My over-excited imagination just wouldn't shut up.

Mark Kermode comes on. He's a well-known British tv personality and he was an important catalyst for this concert to take place. He introduces the band and professes to be an enormous fan. By telling us how the band has strictly forbidden him to use superlatives when saying how great he thinks they are, he is able to make some wild statements and raise anticipation further. Then he asks 'the greatest band in the world' to come on stage. A synthesizer drone is heard and they walk on. They settle behind their respective instruments and wait. And wait, and keep waiting. Oh no! Something seems to be wrong with Steve Fellows' guitar. Please no, please let it be alright... Deep sigh... it is, and they kick off.

The band play – they are careful, conscious, shy – and the music that is *Sleep No More* sounds through the Academy. People smile at their neighbours in recognition. Their eyes light up. And not just their eyes. Their voices are heard. I hear the words to the song coming not only from the stage, but from all around me. There's a deep booming choir standing behind me. Everyone knows the lyrics, is word perfect and eager to sing along. This continues for the entire 90 minutes. The audience know every song by heart and they sometimes sing so loud that Steve is difficult to hear. What a party this is.

I listen, I drink it all in, I smile from ear to ear, I am happy. Oh Lord, it's *Pictures*, it's *Our Secret*, it's *Baby*, it's *Eye Dance*! And I am not at home, listening to my stereo, no, I can see them here in front of me. Steve Fellows, Mik Glaisher, Andy Peake, Kevin Bacon – they're just a few feet away and they play and they sing... and they seem even better than before. Someone please pinch me!

It's hard to believe so many years have passed. How come they seem to play better than ever before? Is this my imagination, have I missed them for so long that I have forgotten how great they used to be and am I now so overwhelmed that I exaggerate what I hear? No, I over-hear comments all around me: 'They sound just stunning, don't they?' and 'Last time I saw them they were already very good, but they seem to have grown'.

Total War begins and I rejoice. Then I feel tears rolling down my cheeks. As I wipe my eyes (because I don't want to cry, I want to be smiling and singing and dancing), I happen to look beside me and see many people make the same wiping movement as I am. I am not the only one crying. And many of the weepers are men. Wow! This is praise for the Comsats indeed. Being able to move people like this.

The entire evening turns out to be an emotional bonding thing. The people who have come here tonight really love the band and they are not afraid to show the world how important this music is to them. The reception they give the Comsats is 500% better than ever before. At first the band don't know how to take this. They start out being nervous, but gradually they relax and find themselves soaking up all that happiness that drifts towards the stage. They grow. They glow. It's almost as if a Happy Balloon is kicked from the audience onto the stage. The band blows a little more air into it and sends it back into the audience. And back to the stage it goes. Every time the balloon changes sides it is a little happier and climbs a little higher. All night it slowly zigzags up to the ceiling.

Shouts come from the audience: 'You're a legend!' and Steve retorts: 'More like a leg-end'. It's hard to be the centre of attention all of a sudden. It's hard to believe you have always been so loved and never knew it.

As to the band themselves, Mik is playing the drums as if his life depends upon it. This man was born to drum. He obviously enjoys himself very much when playing. Kevin's bass playing is tight, and meaty yet subtle, if there is such a thing. I have not seen him play since the eighties and am impressed with what he is doing. Together, Mik and Kevin bring the house down. Such power! Andy the keyboard wizard, who used to be more in the background, now sends in lots of surprising little sounds. He has become more prominent than before and gives the songs extra bits of sparkle. And Steve, who is very tense at the start, visibly relaxes and plays beautifully and sparingly as always. His voice is in fine shape and sometimes sounds better suited to the songs now than on the original records, I think. What a huge victory. Revenge of the Comsats!

A big Thank You to the band for having the courage to play again after such a long time, and playing so incredibly well. And Thank You to the amazing audience who helped them onwards and upwards to heights never reached before.

What made this evening so special was not merely the band having returned with a vengeance after so many years. It was not just that they finally got the admiration and respect they should always have received. It was the combination of this fantastic band, playing awe-inspiring emotional music, being surrounded by their most loyal devotees. The presence of so many people who understood and felt the same, that is what made the gig so memorable. If it didn't sound so scarily American, I might almost use the term 'soul mates'. We were.

This has become rather a raving review, hasn't it? OK, I'll tone it down with some criticism: how dare they not have played *Do the Empty House*? Boo-oo!

(And so I didn't sleep for another week... my over-excited memories just wouldn't shut up.)

Inge

Another four gigs followed. Like old times, October 2009. Ciska, Andy, me and Nahna

An encore

Ernie, do you know you have a banana in your ear?
I'm sorry, Bert, you'll have to speak a little louder. I can't hear you, I have a banana in my ear.

My good friend Bert reads this book carefully and then says: I'm actually still looking for the secret ingredient. What was the attraction of the Comsats, when did lightning strike, why them? Was it the music, was it the boys? Especially since they were a little reluctant at first. I would like to know a little more about the specific appeal of this band. Can you put that into words somehow?

Bert, Bert, listen, Bert.
It was everything. It was a combination.

It was the right band, in the right place, at the right time in my life, when I was just trying to stand on my own two feet, to do my own thing. The right music, which I, without knowing it, was looking for. I don't like superficial stuff, not even then, I like depth. The music of the Comsats was intelligent, well thought out, subtle and full of integrity. Not only was it felt, it was also well thought through. They paid attention to it until it was right. No current trend was copied, no other band was imitated – the music was new and unique. Exactly the direction I wanted to go myself. I didn't want to belong to the masses, I wanted to discover myself, and they wrote the accompanying soundtrack for that. Sparing, clever, profound, and all feeling.

No, I didn't choose them consciously, they crossed my path. Chance had a lot to do with it. If Claire hadn't mentioned them, I might not have discovered the Comsats until much later, if at all. If Mik hadn't written down his home address at our first meeting, things might have turned out differently. If Jive had not been in the audience at that Paradiso gig, the Comsats might not even have existed after the first three records. However, all those things went well, and the band continued, we kept seeing them and gradually became more and more fanatical. So lightning didn't strike at a specific moment, it was a gradually growing process.

It was Steve's lyrics.

Such real questions, fears and emotions. Steve was older than me and therefore further in his development. Over the years I recognised more and more of what he sang about, I learned to name things, I grew up with him. I sucked it all in.

> *You caught me out when you caught me wondering*
> *Just what it is I see in your face*
> *Are you like me, are you feeling out of place?*

It was the lovely people.

The Comsats were all intelligent men, I soon realised that. I was an Anglophile and they were English. I studied English literature at university with great dedication, and they also read books. They had that typical English humour, with a sense of the absurd and full of self-mockery. They were friendly, open and welcoming. Yes, after a short feeling-out period. Call it start-up problems. They weren't used to that much attention from fans, and suddenly there we were, all admiration. They didn't really believe that we could be serious. Who? Us? And then such adoring fans? Yes, until they change their minds, surely.

But we didn't change our minds and the friendship deepened. Right from the start we had all sorts of things in common, from a great love of cats to good food. They couldn't stop talking about those great Dutch 'uitsmijters' (double-fried eggs with ham and cheese) and we drooled over good English cheddar and carrot cake. We became real friends, we shared our lives with each other. They kept track of our studies, jobs and other interests, we got to know their wives and friends, and watched their children and kittens grow up.

It was everything. Earlier in this book I say: 'no Steve, no Comsat Angels'. I would like to supplement this with: no Comsats in my life and I would be a different person now. It really shaped me. I still miss the band a lot. Fortunately, the friendship has remained, still today. All these old people chatting about the good old days!

Made in the USA
Columbia, SC
04 October 2023

23871184R00098